The Ultimate Guide to Rust Programming

Safe, Fast, and Productive Code Discover Rust's powerful features for high-performance applications

THOMPSON CARTER

Table of Content

TABLE OF CONTENTS

Introduction

Mastering Rust: From Systems Programming to Web Development

Rust has swiftly become one of the most sought-after programming languages in modern software development. Known for its combination of **safety**, **performance**, and **concurrency**, Rust is uniquely positioned to tackle a wide range of problems — from low-level systems programming to high-level web development. Its ability to provide fine-grained control over hardware while ensuring memory safety without a garbage collector makes it the perfect tool for building high-performance applications.

This book, *Mastering Rust: From Systems Programming to Web Development*, serves as both a comprehensive guide and a hands-on learning experience for developers eager to explore the full potential of Rust. Whether you are building systems software like operating systems and device drivers, designing fast and reliable web applications, or diving into concurrent programming, this book will guide you through Rust's core features and advanced capabilities, helping you unlock the power of Rust in a wide variety of domains.

Why Rust?

In an era where performance, memory management, and safety are critical in software development, Rust stands out for its strong emphasis on ensuring these qualities while providing developers with the tools they need to write highly efficient, safe, and concurrent code.

- **Memory Safety Without Garbage Collection**: Rust's ownership system ensures that all memory is properly managed at compile time, preventing common issues like **null pointer dereferencing**, **buffer overflows**, and **data races**. This makes it a preferred language for systems-level programming where such issues can have dire consequences.

- **Concurrency Without Fear**: Rust's concurrency model is designed to prevent data races and ensure thread safety. This makes Rust an ideal language for building **multi-threaded applications** and **concurrent services**. It allows developers to write code that can scale across modern multi-core architectures with confidence.

- **Zero-Cost Abstractions**: Rust enables the use of high-level abstractions such as iterators, closures, and async/await without sacrificing performance.

Rust's compiler is capable of optimizing these abstractions down to efficient, low-level code, making Rust a high-performance language that does not compromise on ease of use.

- **Community-Driven and Growing Ecosystem**: With a rapidly growing community and an ever-expanding set of libraries and frameworks, Rust is no longer just for systems programming. From **WebAssembly** (Wasm) to **embedded systems**, Rust's ecosystem is continually evolving to meet the needs of developers in diverse fields.

What You Will Learn in This Book

This book takes a deep dive into **Rust** by covering foundational concepts, advanced programming techniques, and best practices, providing you with a solid understanding of how to write both safe and efficient code. The book is divided into several key sections, each focusing on a distinct area of Rust programming:

Part 1: Fundamentals of Rust Programming

Before diving into more complex topics, we start by grounding you in **Rust's fundamentals**. You'll get an overview of its core features, including:

- **Ownership, Borrowing, and Lifetimes**: These are the cornerstones of Rust's memory safety model, ensuring data is safely accessed and mutated.
- **Basic Syntax and Control Flow**: Learn how to write Rust functions, use conditionals, loops, and pattern matching, and work with data types.
- **Error Handling**: Discover how to manage errors with Rust's `Result` and `Option` types, and understand how to handle exceptions effectively.
- **Testing and Debugging**: Learn how to write unit tests and debug your Rust code using tools like GDB and LLDB.

Part 2: Systems Programming with Rust

Rust shines when it comes to **systems programming**. This section explores:

- **Memory Management**: Go deeper into how Rust manages memory without a garbage collector, and how you can optimize memory usage in your programs.

- **Unsafe Rust**: Understand when and how to use **unsafe Rust** to bypass safety checks for performance-critical or low-level operations.

- **FFI (Foreign Function Interface)**: Learn how to interface with **C libraries**, allowing you to leverage existing C code and integrate Rust with other system-level languages.

- **Writing System Utilities and Kernels**: Discover how to write system-level programs and even develop your own **operating system kernel** in Rust.

Part 3: Web Development with Rust

In this section, we focus on **Rust in web development**, showcasing how to build high-performance web applications:

- **Web Frameworks**: Learn to use **Rocket** and **Actix**, two of Rust's leading web frameworks, to build scalable web services.

- **Building REST APIs**: Step through the process of building and deploying a simple REST API, interacting with databases, and handling HTTP requests and responses.

- **WebSockets for Real-Time Data**: Dive into building **real-time applications** using WebSockets, including chat applications and live data dashboards.

Part 4: Advanced Rust Techniques

Once you are comfortable with Rust's core features, we delve into **advanced techniques**:

- **Zero-Cost Abstractions**: Understand how to write high-level code that compiles into efficient, low-level machine code, optimizing your programs for maximum performance.
- **Concurrency and Parallelism**: Learn Rust's approach to concurrency, handling multi-threading and parallel execution while maintaining memory safety.
- **Optimizing Code for Performance**: Discover best practices for optimizing memory usage, minimizing allocations, and leveraging Rust's efficient data structures.

Part 5: Best Practices and Future Directions

This section explores the **best practices** for writing idiomatic, maintainable, and efficient Rust code, as well as the **future of Rust** and its growing ecosystem. Topics include:

- **Writing Idiomatic Rust**: Learn how to write code that fits naturally within the Rust ecosystem, using idiomatic patterns and conventions.

- **The Rust Community and Ecosystem**: Discover the growing ecosystem of libraries, tools, and frameworks that make Rust an excellent choice for both systems and application-level programming.
- **The Future of Rust**: Gain insights into how Rust is evolving and where the language is headed in the coming years, including its role in **WebAssembly, embedded systems**, and **cloud computing**.

Real-World Example: Building a Large-Scale Project in Rust

In the final section of the book, we apply everything we've learned to **designing and building a large-scale Rust project**. Through a step-by-step guide, we will:

- Design the architecture of a distributed system using Rust.
- Break the project into manageable components and integrate them.
- Use advanced Rust features, such as **async programming**, **concurrency**, and **memory management**, to build a performant and scalable system.

Why This Book Is for You

Whether you're a seasoned developer looking to expand your skills into **systems programming** or a web developer eager to explore Rust's capabilities in building high-performance applications, this book offers something for everyone. It is structured to guide you from **beginner** to **advanced** level, starting with the basics and gradually exploring deeper, more complex topics.

The **real-world examples** and **hands-on exercises** will help you cement your knowledge and gain practical experience, ensuring that you not only understand the concepts but also know how to apply them to solve real problems.

Conclusion

Mastering Rust: From Systems Programming to Web Development is your ultimate guide to becoming proficient in **Rust programming**. This book will equip you with the knowledge and skills you need to harness the power of Rust for systems programming, web development, and performance optimization. As you progress through the chapters, you'll learn how to use Rust's features to write **safe**, **efficient**, and **scalable** code, setting you up for success in the world of modern software development.

Let's embark on this journey together and unlock the full potential of Rust!

CHAPTER 1

INTRODUCTION TO RUST

In this chapter, we'll explore what Rust is, why it has become so popular, and how to set up a development environment to start programming in Rust. We will also walk through the basic syntax and write our very first Rust program, a "Hello, World!" example.

Overview of Rust and Its Rise in Popularity

Rust is a systems programming language that prioritizes safety, speed, and concurrency. It has grown rapidly in popularity, largely due to its ability to deliver performance comparable to C and C++ while avoiding many of their common pitfalls, such as memory safety errors and data races.

Rust's main selling point is its strict memory safety guarantees. It prevents null pointer dereferencing, buffer overflows, and data races, all at compile time. These features make Rust a compelling choice for developing high-performance applications like game engines, web servers, and even operating systems.

The language was originally created by Mozilla Research in 2010 and was designed to address issues in C++ development, particularly memory safety without sacrificing performance. Since then, it has steadily gained a passionate community and is now consistently ranked as one of the most loved programming languages in developer surveys.

Key Features: Memory Safety, Concurrency, and Performance

Rust is built around three core features that make it stand out from many other languages:

1. **Memory Safety:** Rust ensures that programs are free of memory bugs like dangling pointers, buffer overflows, or double frees. This is achieved without relying on a garbage collector, using a concept called ownership. Every piece of data in Rust has a single owner, and when that owner goes out of scope, the data is automatically cleaned up. This approach prevents many common memory issues in other languages.

2. **Concurrency:** Rust has built-in tools for writing concurrent code without the risk of data races. It uses its ownership system to guarantee that only one thread can access a piece of data at a time, eliminating race conditions and making concurrent programming safer and easier.

3. **Performance:** Rust is compiled to native machine code and is designed to be as fast as C and C++ while ensuring safety. It offers fine-grained control over memory allocation and system resources, allowing developers to write high-performance applications that can run on a wide variety of platforms.

Installing Rust and Setting Up the Development Environment

Before we start coding, you'll need to set up the Rust programming language on your computer. Rust's official toolchain manager, **Rustup**, makes it easy to install and manage Rust versions.

Steps to Install Rust:

1. **Install Rustup:**
   o   Go to the official Rust website.

- o Download the installer for your operating system (Windows, macOS, or Linux).
- o Run the installation command. For most systems, it's as simple as running this in your terminal:

```
nginx
```

```
curl --proto '=https' --tlsv1.2 -sSf
https://sh.rustup.rs | sh
```

2. **Verify the Installation:**

- o After installation, open your terminal or command prompt and type:

```
css
```

```
rustc --version
```

This should print out the installed version of the Rust compiler, confirming that Rust has been installed correctly.

3. **Install a Code Editor:**

- o While you can use any text editor, we recommend using **Visual Studio Code (VS Code)** because it has great Rust support through extensions like `rust-analyzer`.

4. **Set Up Cargo:**

   o Cargo is Rust's package manager and build system. It handles dependencies, compiles packages, and runs tests. It's installed automatically with Rustup.

   o To check if Cargo is working, type:

   ```css
   ```

   ```
   cargo --version
   ```

   Cargo will allow you to manage projects and dependencies efficiently as we move forward in the book.

First "Hello, World!" Program and Basic Syntax

Now that we have Rust installed, let's write a basic "Hello, World!" program. This will help you get familiar with Rust's syntax and structure.

1. **Create a New Project:** Open your terminal and create a new project using Cargo:

```
arduino

cargo new hello_world
cd hello_world
```

This will create a new folder named `hello_world` with a basic project structure and a `main.rs` file.

2. **Write the Code:** Open `src/main.rs` in your code editor and write the following code:

```rust
rust

fn main() {
    println!("Hello, World!");
}
```

Here's a breakdown of the code:

- o   `fn main()`: This defines the entry point of the Rust program. Every Rust program must have a `main` function where execution begins.
- o   `println!`: This is a macro (indicated by the `!` symbol) that prints the string to the console. Unlike many other languages, Rust uses macros for common tasks like printing.

3. **Run the Program:** Back in the terminal, run your program with Cargo:

```
arduino
```

```
cargo run
```

You should see the output:

```
Hello, World!
```

Basic Syntax Overview

Before we wrap up the chapter, let's go over some basic Rust syntax:

- **Variables:** In Rust, variables are immutable by default. If you want to make a variable mutable, you must explicitly use the `mut` keyword:

```rust
let x = 5;   // Immutable
let mut y = 10;   // Mutable
```

- **Data Types:** Rust has a variety of data types, including integers (`i32`, `u32`), floating-point numbers (`f32`, `f64`), characters (`char`), and booleans (`bool`).

You can also use more complex types like arrays and tuples.

```rust
```

```rust
let num: i32 = 10;
let decimal: f64 = 3.14;
let flag: bool = true;
let character: char = 'A';
```

- **Comments:** Rust supports both single-line (`//`) and multi-line comments (`/* */`).

```rust
```

```rust
// This is a single-line comment
/* This is a
   multi-line comment */
```

Conclusion

In this chapter, you've been introduced to Rust and its key features like memory safety, concurrency, and performance. You've also set up your Rust development environment and written your first Rust program. In the next chapter, we'll explore Rust's core principles in more detail, particularly its ownership system, which is the backbone of its memory safety features.

Let's move forward and begin writing more complex code!

CHAPTER 2

RUST'S CORE PRINCIPLES

In this chapter, we dive into the fundamental principles that make Rust unique and powerful. Rust is built around its core focus on **memory safety**, **ownership**, and **concurrency**, which are essential for high-performance systems programming. We'll explore how Rust manages memory without a garbage collector, the key concepts of **borrowing**, **references**, and **lifetimes**, and why these features make Rust an excellent choice for systems programming.

Safety and Ownership Model

One of Rust's standout features is its ownership model, which ensures memory safety without the need for a garbage collector. This ownership model is tightly integrated with the language, providing guarantees at compile time that prevent common memory bugs like use-after-free, dangling pointers, and data races.

In Rust, every piece of data has a single **owner** at any point in time. This means that when the owner of a piece of data goes out of scope, Rust will automatically clean up that data, freeing the memory in a safe and predictable manner.

The three core rules of Rust's ownership model are:

1. **Each value in Rust has a variable that's its owner.**
   o When you assign a value to a variable, that variable becomes the owner of the value. The value's memory is freed when the owner goes out of scope.

2. **A value can only have one owner at a time.**
   o If ownership is transferred (through assignment or passing to a function), the previous owner can no longer access that value.

3. **When the owner goes out of scope, the value is dropped.**
   o Rust will automatically release the memory occupied by a value once its owner goes out of scope. This is similar to destructors in other languages but happens automatically.

Here's an example:

```rust

fn main() {
```

```
    let s = String::from("Hello, Rust!");   // s
owns the String
    let t = s;   // Ownership of the String moves
to t
    // println!("{}", s);   // Error: s no longer
owns the String
    println!("{}", t);   // Works fine
}   // t goes out of scope, and memory is freed
```

In this example, when we assign s to t, ownership of the String is moved to t, and s can no longer be used. This ensures that memory is not inadvertently freed or accessed after it's no longer valid.

Borrowing, References, and Lifetimes

While ownership is a key concept, **borrowing** and **references** are central to how Rust allows efficient memory use without unnecessary ing. Rust enables borrowing data through **references**, which allow us to refer to data without taking ownership of it.

There are two types of references in Rust:

1. **Immutable References (&T):**

o Multiple immutable references to a piece of data can exist at the same time. These references allow read-only access to data without modifying it.

rust

```
let s = String::from("Hello");
let r1 = &s;  // First immutable reference
let r2 = &s;  // Second immutable reference
println!("{}, {}", r1, r2);  // Both can be
used simultaneously
```

2. **Mutable References (&mut T):**

o Only one mutable reference to a piece of data can exist at a time. This prevents data races because it ensures that no other references (immutable or mutable) can access the data while it's being mutated.

rust

```
let mut s = String::from("Hello");
let r1 = &mut s;  // Mutable reference
r1.push_str(", Rust!");    // Modify the
value
println!("{}", r1);    // Output: Hello,
Rust!
```

Rust's borrowing system ensures that references are always valid. This is where **lifetimes** come into play.

Understanding Lifetimes

Lifetimes are Rust's way of ensuring that references are valid for as long as they're needed but not longer, preventing dangling references. A **lifetime** is the scope for which a reference is valid, and Rust uses lifetimes to track the relationship between the lifetime of a reference and the lifetime of the data it refers to.

Rust's compiler uses lifetimes to guarantee that references do not outlive the data they point to. If a reference outlives the data it points to, Rust will raise a compile-time error.

Consider this example:

```rust
fn main() {
    let s1 = String::from("Hello");
    let s2 = String::from("Rust");

    let r1 = &s1;  // Immutable reference to s1
    let r2 = &s2;  // Immutable reference to s2
```

```
    println!("{},    {}",   r1,   r2);        //   Both
references are valid
}  // r1 and r2 are dropped here, memory is freed
```

In this case, r1 and r2 are valid for the duration of the function, but once the function ends, the references are no longer valid, and the memory for s1 and s2 is freed.

However, if a reference outlives the data, we'll get an error:

rust

```
fn main() {
    let r;
    {
        let s = String::from("Hello");
        r = &s;    // Error: reference `r` will
outlive `s`
    }  // s goes out of scope, but r is still
trying to access it
    println!("{}", r);  // This is unsafe
}  // Error: reference `r` would be dangling
```

This is a basic example of how lifetimes ensure the safety of references.

Understanding How Rust Manages Memory Without a Garbage Collector

Rust manages memory efficiently without relying on a **garbage collector (GC),** a feature common in languages like Java or Python. Instead of a GC, Rust uses its **ownership** system, combined with **borrowing** and **lifetime** tracking, to manage memory at compile time.

The absence of a garbage collector means that Rust programs don't incur the overhead of garbage collection pauses, which can be significant in high-performance systems. Rust ensures memory safety by enforcing strict rules about ownership, borrowing, and lifetimes during compilation. This leads to more predictable memory usage and less runtime overhead.

Because Rust ensures memory safety at compile time, the need for manual memory management (like in C or C++) is eliminated. Rust's ownership model and memory management approach allow developers to write highly efficient code that is both safe and free of common memory errors, without incurring the runtime cost of garbage collection.

Why Rust is Well-Suited for Systems Programming

Rust is an ideal choice for systems programming for several reasons:

1. **Performance**: Rust compiles to machine code and has performance comparable to C and C++. This makes it suitable for tasks that require low-level system access, such as operating systems, device drivers, and embedded systems.

2. **Memory Safety**: Unlike C/C++, Rust guarantees memory safety at compile time without the need for a garbage collector. This reduces the risk of memory leaks, buffer overflows, and other common low-level memory bugs.

3. **Concurrency**: Rust's ownership model and built-in concurrency features make it easier to write safe and efficient concurrent code. Rust ensures that there are no data races by enforcing ownership rules during compilation.

4. **Zero-cost Abstractions**: Rust provides abstractions that don't come with runtime cost. This means you can write high-level code without sacrificing performance, which is crucial for systems programming.

5. **Tooling and Ecosystem**: Rust comes with robust tools, such as Cargo (for package management and building), `rustfmt` (for code formatting), and `clippy` (for linting), which help maintain high-quality code. The growing Rust ecosystem also includes libraries and frameworks for a wide variety of use cases.

Conclusion

In this chapter, we've covered the core principles that define Rust's safety, performance, and memory management. The ownership model, combined with borrowing, references, and lifetimes, provides Rust with the ability to ensure memory safety without a garbage collector. These features make Rust a powerful choice for systems programming, where performance and safety are paramount. In the next chapter, we'll explore how to work with variables, data types, and functions in Rust to start building more complex programs.

CHAPTER 3

VARIABLES, DATA TYPES, AND FUNCTIONS

In this chapter, we'll dive into the fundamentals of working with **variables**, **data types**, and **functions** in Rust. These are key building blocks that will allow you to structure your programs effectively. We'll explore how to declare variables, understand Rust's primitive types and collections, create and use functions, and handle control flow using conditional statements and loops.

Declaring Variables and Constants

In Rust, variables are immutable by default, meaning their values cannot be changed once set. If you want to make a variable mutable, you need to explicitly use the `mut` keyword.

Immutable Variables:
```rust
rust
```

```rust
fn main() {
```

```
    let x = 5;   // Immutable variable
    // x = 10;   // Error: cannot assign twice to
immutable variable
    println!("x: {}", x);
}
```

In this example, x is immutable. Attempting to reassign x will result in a compile-time error.

Mutable Variables:

To make a variable mutable, we use the mut keyword:

rust

```
fn main() {
    let mut x = 5;   // Mutable variable
    println!("x before: {}", x);
    x = 10;   // Reassigning is allowed because x
is mutable
    println!("x after: {}", x);
}
```

Here, x is mutable, so we can reassign its value.

Constants:

Constants are also declared using const and must have their types explicitly specified. Unlike variables, constants are always immutable and can be set at compile time, not runtime.

```rust
```

```
const MAX_POINTS: u32 = 100_000;   // Constant
declaration
println!("The   maximum   points   are:   {}",
MAX_POINTS);
```

Constants are typically written in uppercase to distinguish them from variables.

Exploring Rust's Primitive Types and Collections

Rust provides a variety of primitive types and collections to handle different kinds of data. Here, we'll explore some of the basic types that you will use frequently in Rust programs.

Primitive Types:

1. **Integer Types**: Rust supports signed and unsigned integers with different bit sizes. The signed types are i8, i16, i32, i64, and i128, while the unsigned types are u8, u16, u32, u64, and u128.

```rust
rust
```

```rust
let a: i32 = 100;   // Signed integer
let b: u32 = 200;   // Unsigned integer
```

2. **Floating Point Types**: Rust provides two floating-point types: f32 and f64, where f64 is the default.

```rust
rust
```

```rust
let pi: f64 = 3.14159;
let e: f32 = 2.71828;
```

3. **Boolean Type**: Rust's bool type has two possible values: true or false.

```rust
rust
```

```rust
let is_rust_awesome: bool = true;
```

4. **Character Type**: Rust's char type represents a single character, and it is stored as a Unicode scalar value.

```rust
rust
```

```rust
let letter: char = 'R';
```

Collections:

Rust includes several types of collections, which allow you to store multiple values. Common collections include **arrays**, **vectors**, and **hash maps**.

1. **Arrays**: Arrays store a fixed number of elements of the same type. The size of the array is known at compile time.

    rust

    ```rust
    let arr: [i32; 3] = [1, 2, 3];
    println!("{}", arr[0]);  // Accessing array element
    ```

2. **Vectors**: Vectors are like arrays but can grow in size. They are more flexible than arrays and are commonly used in Rust programs.

    rust

    ```rust
    let mut v: Vec<i32> = Vec::new();
    v.push(10);    // Add an element to the vector
    v.push(20);
    println!("{}", v[0]);    // Access vector element
    ```

3. **Hash Maps**: Hash maps store key-value pairs. They are useful when you need to look up values by a unique key.

rust

```
use std::collections::HashMap;

let mut map = HashMap::new();
map.insert("key1", 10);
map.insert("key2", 20);
println!("{}", map["key1"]);   // Accessing value by key
```

Functions: Definitions, Parameters, and Return Types

Functions in Rust allow you to group related code into reusable blocks. Functions can accept parameters and return values. Let's go over how to define and use functions in Rust.

Function Definition:

A function is defined using the `fn` keyword followed by the function name and a pair of parentheses for parameters.

rust

```
fn greet() {
```

```
    println!("Hello, Rust!");
}
```

Here, `greet` is a function that takes no parameters and returns nothing.

Functions with Parameters:

You can define functions that accept parameters. Each parameter must have a specified type.

rust

```
fn greet_person(name: &str) {
    println!("Hello, {}!", name);
}
```

In this example, the function `greet_person` takes a `name` of type `&str` (a string slice) as a parameter and prints a greeting.

Functions with Return Values:

Rust functions can return values. The return type is specified after the `->` symbol. The `return` keyword is used to return a value, but if the function ends with an expression, it's implicitly returned.

rust

```
fn add(a: i32, b: i32) -> i32 {
    a + b  // Return is implicit here
}
```

Alternatively, you can explicitly return a value with the `return` keyword:

rust

```
fn multiply(a: i32, b: i32) -> i32 {
    return a * b;
}
```

Control Flow: If, Match, Loops, and Pattern Matching

Control flow is essential in programming to make decisions and repeat tasks. Rust offers several control flow structures like `if` statements, `match` expressions, and various types of loops.

If Statements:

`if` statements in Rust work like in most languages, where you can evaluate expressions and perform actions based on the result.

39

```rust
rust


let number = 10;
if number < 5 {
    println!("Smaller than 5");
} else {
    println!("Greater than or equal to 5");
}
```

You can also use `else if` for more complex conditions:

```rust
rust


let number = 10;
if number < 5 {
    println!("Smaller than 5");
} else if number == 5 {
    println!("Equal to 5");
} else {
    println!("Greater than 5");
}
```

Match Expressions:

Rust's `match` expression is similar to a `switch` statement in other languages but is much more powerful. It allows you to pattern match on values and bind variables from the matched data.

```rust
rust
```

```rust
let number = 5;
match number {
    1 => println!("One"),
    2 => println!("Two"),
    3 | 4 => println!("Three or Four"),
    _ => println!("Other"),
}
```

Here, _ is a wildcard that catches all other possibilities.

Loops:

Rust provides three main types of loops: loop, while, and for.

1. **Infinite Loop** (loop):

   rust

   ```rust
   let mut counter = 0;
   loop {
       println!("Counter: {}", counter);
       counter += 1;
       if counter == 5 {
           break;  // Exits the loop
       }
   }
   ```

2. **While Loop**:

rust

```rust
let mut counter = 0;
while counter < 5 {
    println!("Counter: {}", counter);
    counter += 1;
}
```

3. **For Loop** (often used with collections):

rust

```rust
let arr = [1, 2, 3, 4];
for element in arr.iter() {
    println!("{}", element);
}
```

In this example, iter() creates an iterator over the array, and for allows us to process each element.

Conclusion

In this chapter, we covered the basics of declaring variables and constants, understanding Rust's primitive types and collections, defining functions with parameters and return values, and using control flow mechanisms like `if`, `match`, and loops. These fundamental concepts are essential for writing more complex and efficient programs in Rust.

In the next chapter, we will build on this knowledge by diving deeper into Rust's **ownership model**, **borrowing**, and **memory safety**, which will give you a more thorough understanding of how Rust ensures safe and efficient memory usage.

CHAPTER 4

MEMORY SAFETY IN PRACTICE

In this chapter, we dive into one of the core features that makes Rust stand out: **memory safety**. Rust's strict ownership model, combined with borrowing and references, ensures that memory-related bugs like null pointer dereferencing, buffer overflows, and data races are caught at compile time, rather than during execution. We'll explore ownership in depth, how to manage borrowing and mutable references, and how Rust's compiler solves common memory issues. We'll also look at real-world examples of memory safety in action.

Understanding Ownership In-Depth

At the heart of Rust's memory safety is the **ownership model**. Every piece of data in Rust has an owner, and ownership follows strict rules. Understanding these rules is crucial to mastering memory safety.

The Three Ownership Rules:

1. **Each value in Rust has a variable that is its owner.** When you assign a value to a variable, that variable is responsible for the value. For example, when a variable goes out of scope, its memory is automatically freed.

rust

```
fn main() {
    let s = String::from("Hello, Rust!");
// s owns the String
    // When s goes out of scope, the memory
is freed automatically
}
```

2. **A value can only have one owner at a time.** Ownership can be **transferred**, but it's important to understand that once ownership is transferred, the previous owner can no longer access the value.

rust

```
fn main() {
    let s1 = String::from("Hello");
    let s2 = s1;  // Ownership of the String
moves from s1 to s2
```

45

```
    // println!("{}", s1);   // Error: s1 no
longer owns the String
    println!("{}", s2);   // This works fine
}
```

3. **When the owner goes out of scope, the value is dropped.**

   Rust automatically frees memory when the owner variable goes out of scope, making sure resources are cleaned up without the need for a garbage collector.

   rust

```
fn main() {
    let s = String::from("Goodbye");
    // s will be automatically dropped here
at the end of the scope
}
```

These rules are enforced at **compile time**, so you don't have to worry about memory being freed at the wrong time, and you also avoid the risk of accidental use of freed memory.

Managing Borrowing and Mutable References

While ownership is crucial for memory safety, **borrowing** allows for more flexibility. Rust lets you **borrow** data through references, which allow multiple parts of your code to access the same data safely.

Immutable References (&T):

You can borrow data immutably, meaning the data can be read but not modified. Multiple immutable references to a piece of data can coexist.

```rust
fn main() {
    let s = String::from("Hello, Rust!");
    let r1 = &s;  // First immutable reference
    let r2 = &s;  // Second immutable reference
    println!("r1: {}, r2: {}", r1, r2);  // Both
can be used simultaneously
}
```

Mutable References (&mut T):

A **mutable reference** allows you to modify the borrowed data. However, Rust guarantees that there can only be one mutable reference to a piece of data at a time, preventing race conditions and ensuring exclusive access.

rust

```
fn main() {
    let mut s = String::from("Hello");
    let r1 = &mut s;  // First mutable reference
    r1.push_str(", Rust!");   // Modify the data
through r1
    println!("{}", r1);   // Output: Hello, Rust!
}
```

Attempting to create a second mutable reference at the same time would cause a compile-time error:

rust

```
fn main() {
    let mut s = String::from("Hello");
    let r1 = &mut s;  // First mutable reference
    let r2 = &mut s;  // Error: cannot borrow `s`
as mutable more than once
    println!("{}", r1);
}
```

Combining Mutable and Immutable References:

Rust ensures that you cannot have mutable and immutable references to the same data simultaneously, which could cause undefined behavior in other languages. This is a key feature that prevents data races and ensures safety.

rust

```
fn main() {
    let mut s = String::from("Hello");
    let r1 = &s;  // Immutable reference
    let r2 = &mut s;  // Error: cannot borrow `s`
as mutable because it is also borrowed as
immutable
    println!("{}", r1);
}
```

This strict rule ensures that data is either being read by multiple parts of the code (immutable) or modified exclusively by one part (mutable), but never both.

Solving Common Memory Issues with Rust's Compiler

Rust's **borrow checker** is a key component that ensures memory safety. It analyzes the ownership and borrowing rules at compile time and prevents common memory-related issues like **dangling pointers**, **double frees**, and **race conditions**.

Dangling Pointers:

A dangling pointer occurs when a pointer refers to memory that has already been freed. This can lead to unpredictable behavior and crashes in programs. Rust prevents this by ensuring that references cannot outlive the data they point to.

For example:

```rust
fn main() {
    let s: String;
    {
        let temp = String::from("Hello");
        s = &temp;  // Error: temporary value is dropped here
    }
    println!("{}", s);  // Error: s is a dangling reference
}
```

Rust ensures that references cannot outlive the data they refer to by enforcing lifetimes, which we'll discuss in a later chapter.

Double Frees:

Rust prevents double frees by enforcing its ownership rules. When ownership of data is transferred, the previous owner can no longer access or attempt to free the data.

rust

```
fn main() {
    let s1 = String::from("Hello");
    let s2 = s1;  // Ownership moves to s2
    // drop(s1);  // Error: s1 no longer owns the
String
}
```

Since s1 no longer owns the String, calling drop(s1) would result in a compile-time error, preventing double frees.

Data Races:

Rust's ownership and borrowing model also prevents **data races** in concurrent programming. A data race happens when two or more threads access the same memory location simultaneously, and at least one of them modifies the data.

Rust ensures that data can be either:

- Accessed immutably by many threads, but not modified
- Accessed mutably by exactly one thread, ensuring that no other threads can access it at the same time

```rust
rust

use std::thread;

fn main() {
    let mut data = String::from("Hello");

    let handle = thread::spawn(move || {
        data.push_str(", world!");
        println!("{}", data);    // Error: can't
move data into the thread
    });

    handle.join().unwrap();
    // println!("{}", data);    // Error: data
moved to the thread
}
```

In this example, data is moved into the thread and can no longer be accessed by the main thread. This ensures there's no possibility of a race condition.

Real-World Examples of Memory Safety

1. **Building a File System Scanner:** Let's say you're building a program to scan files and directories for specific patterns. Using Rust's ownership system, you can safely manage memory when reading from files.

```rust
use std::fs::File;
use std::io::{self, Read};

fn read_file(file_path: &str) -> io::Result<String> {
    let mut file = File::open(file_path)?;
    let mut contents = String::new();
    file.read_to_string(&mut contents)?;
    Ok(contents)
}

fn main() {
    let path = "sample.txt";
    match read_file(path) {
        Ok(contents) => println!("File contents:\n{}", contents),
        Err(e) => eprintln!("Error reading file: {}", e),
    }
```

```
}
```

In this example, `file` is borrowed to read the contents of the file safely, and once `file` goes out of scope, the memory is freed automatically.

2. **Web Server Handling Concurrent Requests:** Consider a web server that handles incoming requests concurrently. Using Rust's ownership and borrowing rules, we can ensure that multiple threads accessing shared data do so safely.

rust

```
use std::sync::{Arc, Mutex};
use std::thread;

fn                     handle_request(data:
Arc<Mutex<String>>) {
    let mut data = data.lock().unwrap();
    data.push_str(" - Request Handled");
    println!("{}", *data);
}

fn main() {
    let           data           =
Arc::new(Mutex::new(String::from("Request
data")));
```

```
let threads: Vec<_> = (0..5).map(|_| {
    let data = Arc::clone(&data);
    thread::spawn(move || {
        handle_request(data);
    })
}).collect();

for t in threads {
    t.join().unwrap();
}
}
```

The `Arc<Mutex<T>>` combination allows safe concurrent access to shared data, ensuring that only one thread can mutate the data at a time.

Conclusion

In this chapter, we explored Rust's approach to **memory safety** through its ownership model, borrowing, and mutable references. Rust's compiler ensures memory safety by enforcing strict rules that prevent common memory issues like dangling pointers, double frees, and data races. Through real-world examples, we saw how Rust's ownership model helps build safe, efficient systems while minimizing runtime errors. In the next chapter, we will explore more advanced memory management techniques and dive deeper into **lifetime** concepts, which are essential to understanding how references and borrowing work in Rust.

CHAPTER 5

STRUCTS AND ENUMS

In this chapter, we'll explore two of the most powerful data structures in Rust: **structs** and **enums**. These are essential for organizing data in a way that models real-world concepts and relationships. Structs are used to define custom data types that group related data together, while enums allow us to define types that can represent different possible values. We will also explore how to implement methods for structs and how to use enums for flexible, readable code.

Defining and Using Structs

A **struct** in Rust is a custom data type that lets you group related values (fields) together. You can think of structs as a way to create complex objects that have properties (fields) and behavior (methods).

Basic Structs:

A basic struct is defined using the `struct` keyword followed by the name of the struct and its fields:

```rust
struct Person {
    name: String,
    age: u32,
}

fn main() {
    let person1 = Person {
        name: String::from("Alice"),
        age: 30,
    };
    println!("Name: {}, Age: {}", person1.name,
person1.age);
}
```

Here, the `Person` struct has two fields: `name` and `age`. We create an instance of `Person` called `person1`, initializing it with values for `name` and `age`.

Tuple Structs:

Rust also allows you to define tuple structs, which are like regular structs, but instead of naming each field, you simply define them by their order. Tuple structs are often used when you want a lightweight, unnamed type:

```rust
```

```
struct Point(i32, i32);

fn main() {
    let point = Point(10, 20);
    println!("Point    coordinates:    ({},    {})",
point.0, point.1);
}
```

In this example, `Point` is a tuple struct that stores two `i32` values, and we access them by index (`point.0` and `point.1`).

The Power of Enums for Flexible Code

Enums (short for "enumerations") are another powerful feature in Rust that allows you to define a type that can have multiple different values. Enums are particularly useful when you need to represent a value that can be one of several possibilities, often making your code more readable and concise.

Basic Enums:

To define an enum, use the `enum` keyword followed by the name of the enum and its variants:

59

rust

```rust
enum Direction {
    Up,
    Down,
    Left,
    Right,
}


fn move_player(direction: Direction) {
    match direction {
        Direction::Up => println!("Moving up"),
        Direction::Down   =>   println!("Moving down"),
        Direction::Left   =>   println!("Moving left"),
        Direction::Right   =>   println!("Moving right"),
    }
}

fn main() {
    let direction = Direction::Up;
    move_player(direction);
}
```

In this example, the Direction enum defines four variants: Up, Down, Left, and Right. The move_player function uses a `match` statement to check the direction and perform an action accordingly.

Enums with Data:

Enums in Rust can also store data with each variant, which makes them extremely flexible. This is especially useful when different variants need to carry different types of data:

```rust
rust

enum Message {
    Quit,
    Move { x: i32, y: i32 },
    Write(String),
}

fn process_message(message: Message) {
    match message {
        Message::Quit                        =>
println!("Quitting..."),
        Message::Move    {    x,    y    }   =>
println!("Moving to ({}, {})", x, y),
        Message::Write(text)                 =>
println!("Writing: {}", text),
    }
}

fn main() {
```

```
    let msg1 = Message::Move { x: 10, y: 20 };
    let              msg2              =
Message::Write(String::from("Hello, Rust!"));
    process_message(msg1);
    process_message(msg2);
}
```

In this case, the `Message` enum has three variants: `Quit`, `Move` (which stores two `i32` values), and `Write` (which stores a `String`). The `match` expression is used to handle each variant, and each variant is processed differently based on the data it contains.

Implementing Methods for Structs Using `impl`

Rust allows you to associate methods with structs, making them more useful and flexible. The `impl` block is used to define methods for a struct, including constructors, accessors, and other helper functions.

Implementing Methods:

rust

```
struct Circle {
    radius: f64,
}
```

```rust
impl Circle {
    // Constructor method
    fn new(radius: f64) -> Circle {
        Circle { radius }
    }

    // Method to calculate the area of the circle
    fn area(&self) -> f64 {
        std::f64::consts::PI * self.radius * self.radius
    }

    // Method to change the radius of the circle
    fn set_radius(&mut self, radius: f64) {
        self.radius = radius;
    }
}

fn main() {
    let mut circle = Circle::new(5.0);  // Using the constructor
    println!("Area: {}", circle.area());    // Calculating the area
    circle.set_radius(10.0);    // Changing the radius
    println!("New Area: {}", circle.area());
}
```

Here, we define the `Circle` struct and implement methods on it using `impl`. The `new` method acts as a constructor, while `area` calculates the area of the circle based on its radius. The `set_radius` method allows us to change the radius of the circle.

Method Receiver Types:

In the above example, we used `&self` (an immutable reference to the instance) and `&mut self` (a mutable reference). These are the most common receiver types for methods:

- `&self` is used for methods that don't modify the instance.
- `&mut self` is used for methods that modify the instance.

In the `area` method, we don't modify the instance, so we use `&self`. In `set_radius`, we need to modify the `radius`, so we use `&mut self`.

Practical Examples: Representing Real-World Objects with Structs and Enums

Let's now look at a practical example of how you might use structs and enums to represent real-world objects in Rust.

We'll model a simple **library system** that involves books and users.

Modeling a Library System:

rust

```rust
// Struct representing a book
struct Book {
    title: String,
    author: String,
    available: bool,
}

impl Book {
    fn new(title: &str, author: &str) -> Book {
        Book {
            title: String::from(title),
            author: String::from(author),
            available: true,
        }
    }

    fn borrow(&mut self) {
        if self.available {
            self.available = false;
            println!("You      borrowed      {}",
self.title);
        } else {
```

```rust
            println!("{} is already borrowed.",
self.title);
        }
    }

    fn return_book(&mut self) {
        self.available = true;
        println!("You returned {}", self.title);
    }
}

// Enum representing different actions in the
library system
enum LibraryAction {
    Borrow(Book),
    Return(Book),
    QueryAvailability(Book),
}

fn perform_action(action: LibraryAction) {
    match action {
        LibraryAction::Borrow(mut    book)    =>
book.borrow(),
        LibraryAction::Return(mut    book)    =>
book.return_book(),
        LibraryAction::QueryAvailability(book)
=> {
            if book.available {
```

```rust
                println!("{}    is    available",
book.title);
            } else {
                println!("{} is not available",
book.title);
            }
        }
    }
}

fn main() {
    let mut book1 = Book::new("1984", "George
Orwell");
    let mut book2 = Book::new("To Kill a
Mockingbird", "Harper Lee");

    // Query availability

perform_action(LibraryAction::QueryAvailability
(book1));

perform_action(LibraryAction::QueryAvailability
(book2));

    // Borrow and return books

perform_action(LibraryAction::Borrow(book1));

perform_action(LibraryAction::Return(book1));
```

```
// Query availability again
```

```
perform_action(LibraryAction::QueryAvailability
(book1));
}
```

In this example, we have:

- A `Book` struct that holds information about a book (title, author, availability) and methods to borrow and return the book.
- A `LibraryAction` enum that represents different actions that can be performed on a book, such as borrowing, returning, or querying availability.
- The `perform_action` function processes these actions using a `match` statement to decide what to do based on the type of action.

This example demonstrates how structs and enums can work together to model complex real-world systems in a clear and flexible way.

Conclusion

In this chapter, we've covered how to define and use **structs** and **enums** in Rust, two powerful data types for building complex programs. We've also explored how to implement methods for structs using the `impl` block to add behavior to our data types. By combining structs and enums, we can represent real-world objects and actions, making our code both flexible and easy to understand. In the next chapter, we'll dive deeper into **error handling** in Rust and explore how to manage errors effectively using `Result` and `Option` types.

CHAPTER 6

ERROR HANDLING WITH RUST

Error handling is one of the most critical parts of building reliable software. In this chapter, we will explore how Rust handles errors in a way that is both **safe** and **efficient**. We will cover the `Result` and `Option` types, which are the main ways Rust handles errors. We will also look at methods like `unwrap` and `expect`, and discuss how to handle errors effectively in production code. Finally, we'll apply these concepts in a **real-world example** of error handling in file I/O operations.

Result and Option Types for Error Handling

In Rust, the standard way to handle errors is by using the **`Result`** and **`Option`** types. These types allow you to explicitly handle success and failure cases rather than relying on exceptions or other error-prone mechanisms.

The `Result` Type:

The `Result` type is used for functions that can return an error. It is an **enum** with two variants:

- **Ok(T)** : Represents a successful result, containing the value of type `T`.
- **Err(E)** : Represents an error, containing an error of type E.

rust

```rust
enum Result<T, E> {
    Ok(T),
    Err(E),
}
```

For example, if you are reading from a file, a function might return a `Result` to indicate whether it was successful or if there was an error reading the file.

rust

```rust
use std::fs::File;
use std::io::{self, Read};

fn read_file(file_path: &str) -> Result<String,
io::Error> {
```

```
    let mut file = File::open(file_path)?; // If
opening fails, it returns Err
    let mut content = String::new();
    file.read_to_string(&mut content)?;
    Ok(content)
}
```

In this case, `File::open()` and `read_to_string()` return a `Result`, and the `?` operator propagates errors by returning `Err` if something goes wrong.

The `Option` Type:

The `Option` type is used for values that may or may not exist. It's an enum with two variants:

- **Some(T)** : Contains a value of type `T`.
- **None**: Represents the absence of a value.

rust

```
enum Option<T> {
    Some(T),
    None,
}
```

You might use `Option` when a value is expected to possibly be missing, such as looking up a key in a map.

rust

```rust
fn find_name(id: u32) -> Option<String> {
    let names = vec!["Alice", "Bob", "Charlie"];
    if id < names.len() as u32 {
        Some(names[id as usize].to_string())
    } else {
        None
    }
}
```

Here, the function returns `Some(name)` if the `id` exists in the vector, or `None` if it doesn't.

The unwrap *and* expect *Methods*

In Rust, functions that return `Result` or `Option` types need to be explicitly handled. However, for cases where you're certain an operation will succeed (for example, when you expect a value to be present), you can use the `unwrap` or `expect` methods.

unwrap:

The `unwrap` method is a shortcut that either returns the value inside an `Ok` or `Some`, or it **panics** if the result is an `Err` or `None`.

rust

```
let result: Result<i32, &str> = Ok(10);
let value = result.unwrap(); // value is 10

let error: Result<i32, &str> = Err("An error
occurred");
let value = error.unwrap(); // This will panic:
thread 'main' panicked at 'An error occurred'
```

While `unwrap` is convenient, it should be used cautiously. If the result is `Err` or `None`, the program will panic and stop execution, which is often not ideal in production environments.

expect:

`expect` works similarly to `unwrap`, but it allows you to provide a custom error message, making it easier to understand the cause of the panic.

rust

```
let result: Result<i32, &str> = Ok(10);
let value = result.expect("Failed to get value");
// value is 10

let error: Result<i32, &str> = Err("An error
occurred");
let value = error.expect("Something went
wrong!"); // This will panic with the message
"Something went wrong!"
```

`expect` is preferred over `unwrap` when you want to give a more descriptive message about why a panic occurred.

Handling Errors Effectively in Production Code

While `unwrap` and `expect` are useful during development, they are **not ideal for production code** because they cause the program to panic when things go wrong. In production, you should handle errors gracefully, ensuring that your program can recover from failures or provide meaningful feedback to the user.

Graceful Error Handling:

Instead of unwrapping results, you can use the `match` statement to handle both success and error cases explicitly:

rust

```rust
fn read_file(file_path: &str) -> Result<String, io::Error> {
    let mut file = File::open(file_path);

    match file {
        Ok(mut f) => {
            let mut content = String::new();
            f.read_to_string(&mut content)?;
            Ok(content)
        }
        Err(e) => Err(e),    // Handle the error explicitly
    }
}
```

In this example, we use `match` to differentiate between `Ok` and `Err`, allowing us to handle errors in a controlled way.

Propagating Errors with the ? Operator:

Rust's ? operator provides a concise way to propagate errors without having to match on them manually. If the result is Err, the error is returned immediately from the function.

rust

```rust
fn read_file(file_path: &str) -> Result<String,
io::Error> {
    let mut file = File::open(file_path)?;   //
Propagate the error if any
    let mut content = String::new();
    file.read_to_string(&mut content)?;
    Ok(content)
}
```

The ? operator makes the code cleaner by automatically returning errors, so you don't need to write boilerplate match statements. However, the function signature must still specify that it returns a Result.

Real-World Example: Error Handling in File I/O Operations

In this section, we'll apply our understanding of error handling to a **real-world file I/O operation**. We'll write a program that reads a file, processes its contents, and handles any potential errors along the way.

Example: Reading and Writing to Files

rust

```rust
use std::fs::File;
use std::io::{self, Read, Write};

fn read_file(file_path: &str) -> Result<String,
io::Error> {
    let mut file = File::open(file_path)?;
    let mut content = String::new();
    file.read_to_string(&mut content)?;
    Ok(content)
}

fn write_file(file_path: &str, content: &str) ->
Result<(), io::Error> {
    let mut file = File::create(file_path)?;
    file.write_all(content.as_bytes())?;
    Ok(())
}

fn main() {
    let file_path = "test.txt";

    // Try to read from a file
    match read_file(file_path) {
```

```
        Ok(content)  => println!("File content:
{}", content),
        Err(e) => eprintln!("Error reading file:
{}", e),
    }

    // Try to write to a file
    let new_content = "Hello, Rust!";
    match write_file("output.txt", new_content)
{
        Ok(_) => println!("Successfully wrote to
the file"),
        Err(e)  => eprintln!("Error  writing  to
file: {}", e),
    }
}
```

In this program:

- The `read_file` function attempts to read the content of a file, returning a `Result` with either the file contents (`Ok`) or an error (`Err`).
- The `write_file` function attempts to write to a file, similarly returning a `Result` to indicate success or failure.
- In the `main` function, we use `match` to handle the success or failure of these file operations and print appropriate messages.

If an error occurs (e.g., the file does not exist or is not accessible), we handle it by printing an error message to the user.

Conclusion

In this chapter, we covered how Rust handles errors using the `Result` and `Option` types, the methods `unwrap` and `expect`, and how to handle errors effectively in production code. We learned that while `unwrap` and `expect` are useful for quick prototyping, they should be avoided in favor of more robust error handling techniques like `match` and the `?` operator. The real-world example of file I/O operations demonstrated how to gracefully handle errors while reading and writing files. In the next chapter, we'll explore how to work with **collections** and **iterators** to manage and manipulate data effectively.

CHAPTER 7

COLLECTIONS AND ITERATORS

In this chapter, we will dive into some of Rust's most powerful features for managing data: **collections** and **iterators**. Collections in Rust, such as arrays, vectors, hash maps, and sets, allow us to store and organize data in various ways. Iterators enable us to efficiently process these collections, providing a clean and concise way to work with large datasets. We'll cover how to manipulate collections, iterate over them, and apply techniques that allow for efficient data handling. Finally, we'll explore a real-world example where we manage **user data** using collections.

Arrays, Vectors, Hash Maps, and Sets

Rust offers a variety of collection types, each suited to different use cases. Let's explore the most common ones:

Arrays:

An **array** is a fixed-size collection that stores elements of the same type. The size of an array must be known at compile time.

rust

```
fn main() {
    let arr: [i32; 3] = [1, 2, 3];
    println!("First element: {}", arr[0]);
}
```

Arrays are simple and fast because their size is known at compile time. However, their size cannot be changed once they are created.

Vectors:

A **vector** (Vec<T>) is a dynamically-sized collection that grows as needed. Vectors are a more flexible alternative to arrays and are widely used in Rust when you need a collection that can grow or shrink.

rust

```
fn main() {
    let mut v: Vec<i32> = Vec::new();
```

```
    v.push(1);
    v.push(2);
    v.push(3);
    println!("First element: {}", v[0]);
}
```

Vectors are used when you need a collection that can dynamically resize. They are particularly useful for storing collections of unknown or variable size.

Hash Maps:

A **hash map** (HashMap<K, V>) stores key-value pairs, where each key maps to a value. It provides fast lookups based on the key. The keys must implement the Eq and Hash traits, and the values can be of any type.

rust

```
use std::collections::HashMap;

fn main() {
    let mut map = HashMap::new();
    map.insert("name", "Alice");
    map.insert("age", "30");
    println!("Name: {}", map["name"]);
}
```

Hash maps are useful when you need to associate keys with values and need fast access to the data.

Sets:

A **set** is an unordered collection that does not allow duplicates. Rust's standard library provides the `HashSet` type, which is part of the `std::collections` module.

rust

```
use std::collections::HashSet;

fn main() {
    let mut set: HashSet<i32> = HashSet::new();
    set.insert(1);
    set.insert(2);
    set.insert(3);
    println!("Set     contains     2:     {}",
set.contains(&2));
}
```

Sets are useful when you want to store unique values and don't care about the order of the elements.

Iterating Over Collections with Iterators

Rust's **iterators** allow you to traverse over collections and apply operations to the elements in a clean and efficient way. Rust iterators are lazy, meaning they only compute values when they are needed, which can help improve performance in certain scenarios.

Using the iter() Method:

The iter() method allows you to iterate over a collection. It returns an iterator, which you can use to apply various operations like map, filter, and for_each.

rust

```rust
fn main() {
    let v = vec![1, 2, 3, 4, 5];

    // Iterating over the vector
    for &x in v.iter() {
        println!("{}", x);
    }
}
```

In this example, iter() creates an iterator that allows us to loop through each element in the vector.

Using the `map()` Method:

The `map()` method transforms each element of the iterator by applying a function.

rust

```rust
fn main() {
    let v = vec![1, 2, 3, 4, 5];

    // Multiply each element by 2 using map()
    let v2: Vec<i32> = v.iter().map(|x| x * 2).collect();

    println!("{:?}", v2);   // Output: [2, 4, 6, 8, 10]
}
```

Here, `map()` takes a closure that multiplies each element by 2, and `collect()` is used to gather the results into a new vector.

Using the `filter()` Method:

The `filter()` method allows you to select elements based on a condition.

rust

```
fn main() {
    let v = vec![1, 2, 3, 4, 5];

    // Select even numbers using filter()
    let evens: Vec<i32> = v.iter().filter(|&&x|
x % 2 == 0).collect();

    println!("{:?}", evens);  // Output: [2, 4]
}
```

`filter()` takes a closure that returns `true` for elements you want to keep, and `false` for those you want to exclude.

Using the `for_each()` Method:

The `for_each()` method applies a function to each element of the iterator.

rust

```
fn main() {
    let v = vec![1, 2, 3, 4, 5];

    v.iter().for_each(|&x|  println!("{}",  x));
// Prints each element
}
```

In this example, `for_each()` is used to print each element of the vector.

Efficient Collection Manipulation Techniques

Rust's iterators are not just for iterating over collections; they also allow for **efficient data manipulation**. Here are a few key techniques for efficiently working with collections:

Chaining Iterators:

You can chain multiple iterator methods to perform complex operations in a concise and efficient way.

rust

```
fn main() {
    let v = vec![1, 2, 3, 4, 5];

    let result: Vec<i32> = v.iter()
                            .map(|&x| x * 2)
                            .filter(|&x| x > 5)
                            .collect();

    println!("{:?}", result);   // Output: [6, 8,
10]
}
```

Here, we first multiply each element by 2, and then filter out values that are not greater than 5. This combination of operations is both efficient and readable.

Reducing Collections:

The `fold()` method allows you to reduce a collection into a single value by applying a binary operation.

rust

```
fn main() {
    let v = vec![1, 2, 3, 4, 5];

    let sum: i32 = v.iter().fold(0, |acc, &x| acc
+ x);

    println!("Sum: {}", sum);   // Output: 15
}
```

`fold()` iterates through the collection and accumulates the result by applying the closure to each element.

Real-World Example: Managing User Data with Collections

Let's put everything together with a practical example: managing **user data** using Rust's collections. We'll use a vector to store users, a hash map to store additional data about them, and iterators to process the data.

```rust

use std::collections::HashMap;

#[derive(Debug)]
struct User {
    id: u32,
    name: String,
    age: u32,
}

fn main() {
    // Create some sample users
    let users = vec![
        User { id: 1, name: String::from("Alice"), age: 30 },
        User { id: 2, name: String::from("Bob"), age: 25 },
        User { id: 3, name: String::from("Charlie"), age: 35 },
    ];

    // Create a HashMap to store user data (e.g., favorite color)
    let mut user_data: HashMap<u32, String> = HashMap::new();
```

```
user_data.insert(1, String::from("Blue"));
user_data.insert(2, String::from("Green"));
user_data.insert(3, String::from("Red"));

// Use iterators to process the user data
let users_over_30: Vec<&User> = users.iter().filter(|&user| user.age > 30).collect();
println!("Users over 30: {:?}", users_over_30);

// Print each user's name and favorite color
for user in &users {
    if let Some(color) = user_data.get(&user.id) {
        println!("User: {}, Favorite Color: {}", user.name, color);
    }
}
}
```

In this example:

- We define a `User` struct to represent user data.
- We use a `Vec<User>` to store a list of users and a `HashMap<u32, String>` to store user data like their favorite color.
- We use the `iter()` and `filter()` methods to find users who are older than 30.

- Finally, we use the `for` loop to print each user's name along with their favorite color.

Conclusion

In this chapter, we've covered how to work with Rust's **collections** like arrays, vectors, hash maps, and sets, and how to iterate over them efficiently using **iterators**. We've also explored how to chain iterator methods and apply efficient manipulation techniques like `map`, `filter`, and `fold`. Using these tools, we can effectively manage and process data in our programs. In the next chapter, we'll explore **error handling** in more detail and learn how to handle errors gracefully in real-world applications.

CHAPTER 8

MODULES AND PACKAGES IN RUST

In this chapter, we'll delve into how Rust's **module system** allows you to organize your code into manageable units and how you can use **Cargo** and **crates** to manage larger projects. Modules help you encapsulate related functionality, while packages allow you to distribute your code as libraries or executables. We'll also explore a **real-world example** of building a modular Command-Line Interface (CLI) application.

Understanding Rust's Module System

Rust's module system helps you organize your code and control its visibility and scope. A **module** in Rust is a collection of functions, structs, enums, and other items grouped together. It helps to separate code into logical parts and promotes reusability.

Defining Modules:

You can define a module using the mod keyword:

```rust
mod greetings {
    pub fn say_hello() {
        println!("Hello, world!");
    }

    fn say_goodbye() {
        println!("Goodbye, world!");
    }
}

fn main() {
    greetings::say_hello();    // This works
because it's public
    // greetings::say_goodbye(); // This will
cause an error because it's private
}
```

Here, the greetings module contains two functions. One is public (pub), and the other is private. The pub keyword makes an item accessible from outside the module, while private items are only accessible within the module itself.

Nested Modules:

Modules can be nested inside other modules. To access a nested module, you use the full path:

rust

```
mod outer {
    pub mod inner {
        pub fn hello() {
            println!("Hello    from    the    inner
module!");
        }
    }
}

fn main() {
    outer::inner::hello();    //    Accessing    the
nested module
}
```

In this example, the `inner` module is nested within the `outer` module, and we access it using the path `outer::inner::hello()`.

File-Based Modules:

In larger projects, it's common to organize modules into separate files. If a module grows large, you can create a separate file for it. The module name matches the filename.

rust

```rust
// In `src/greetings.rs`
pub fn say_hello() {
    println!("Hello, world!");
}


// In `src/main.rs`
mod greetings;  // Import the greetings module

fn main() {
    greetings::say_hello();  // Call the function
from greetings.rs
}
```

By using mod greetings;, Rust will look for a file named greetings.rs in the src directory and import it as a module.

Creating and Importing Libraries

Rust allows you to create libraries and packages that can be shared across multiple projects. Libraries are typically packaged into **crates** and can be reused by importing them into your project.

Creating a Library:

To create a library in Rust, you define a `lib.rs` file in the `src` directory.

rust

```
// In `src/lib.rs`
pub fn add(a: i32, b: i32) -> i32 {
    a + b
}
```

In your `Cargo.toml` file, you define the package as a library (this is the default):

toml

```
[package]
name = "my_library"
version = "0.1.0"
edition = "2018"
```

```
[dependencies]
```

Using External Libraries (Crates):

Rust's package manager, **Cargo**, allows you to include external libraries, or **crates**, in your project. You can add crates to your project by modifying the `Cargo.toml` file.

For example, to use the `serde` crate for serializing and deserializing data, you would add the following to `Cargo.toml`:

```toml
```

```
[dependencies]
serde = "1.0"
```

Then, in your code, you can import and use the crate:

```rust
```

```rust
use serde::{Serialize, Deserialize};

#[derive(Serialize, Deserialize)]
struct Person {
    name: String,
    age: u32,
}
```

Cargo handles downloading, compiling, and linking the external crate to your project.

Organizing Large Projects with Cargo and Crates

Cargo is the Rust package manager and build system, and it's essential for organizing large projects. It handles project dependencies, compiling, testing, and documentation. It makes it easy to create new projects, manage libraries, and distribute your code.

Creating a New Project with Cargo:

To start a new project with Cargo, you can run:

```bash
bash
```

```
cargo new my_project
```

This will create a new directory with the default Rust project structure, including `Cargo.toml`, `src/main.rs`, and other necessary files.

Cargo's `Cargo.toml` File:

The `Cargo.toml` file is where you declare the dependencies, project version, and other configuration for your project. Here's an example:

toml

```
[package]
name = "my_project"
version = "0.1.0"
edition = "2018"

[dependencies]
serde = "1.0"
```

In this example, `serde` is added as a dependency.

Working with Multiple Crates in a Workspace:

In larger projects, you can use a **Cargo workspace** to manage multiple related crates. A workspace is a set of packages that share the same `Cargo.lock` file and output directory. This makes managing dependencies and building multiple crates together easier.

To create a workspace, organize your project directory like this:

```css
my_workspace/
    Cargo.toml
    crate1/
        Cargo.toml
        src/
            lib.rs
    crate2/
        Cargo.toml
        src/
            lib.rs
```

In the root `Cargo.toml`, declare the workspace:

```toml
[workspace]
members = ["crate1", "crate2"]
```

Cargo will then treat all the crates as part of the same workspace, simplifying the build process.

Real-World Example: Building a Modular CLI Application

Now, let's apply the concepts we've learned by building a simple **modular CLI application** that performs basic tasks such as adding users and listing them. We'll organize the project into separate modules and use Cargo to manage it.

1. Create a new project:
bash

```
cargo new user_manager
cd user_manager
```

2. Define the modules:

Inside `src/`, we'll create two modules: `user.rs` (for user data) and `cli.rs` (for handling the command-line interface).

- **src/user.rs** (for managing user data):

rust

```
pub struct User {
    pub name: String,
    pub age: u32,
}

impl User {
    pub fn new(name: String, age: u32) -> User {
        User { name, age }
    }
}
```

- **src/cli.rs** (for handling user commands):

```rust
use crate::user::User;
use std::collections::HashMap;

pub fn add_user(users: &mut HashMap<String,
User>, name: String, age: u32) {
    let user = User::new(name, age);
    users.insert(name.clone(), user);
    println!("Added user: {}", name);
}

pub fn list_users(users: &HashMap<String, User>)
{
    for user in users.values() {
        println!("Name: {}, Age: {}", user.name,
user.age);
    }
}
```

3. Organize the `main.rs` file:

In the `main.rs` file, we'll import our modules and interact with them to perform tasks:

```rust
mod user;
mod cli;
```

```rust
use std::collections::HashMap;

fn main() {
    let mut users = HashMap::new();

    cli::add_user(&mut                    users,
String::from("Alice"), 30);
    cli::add_user(&mut                    users,
String::from("Bob"), 25);

    println!("\nUsers in the system:");
    cli::list_users(&users);
}
```

4. Run the application:

```bash
bash

cargo run
```

This will output:

```yaml
yaml

Added user: Alice
Added user: Bob

Users in the system:
Name: Alice, Age: 30
Name: Bob, Age: 25
```

Conclusion

In this chapter, we've explored how to organize your Rust code using **modules** to group related functions and structs, and how to manage large projects with **Cargo** and **crates**. By using modules, you can keep your code clean and modular, which is particularly useful as your project grows. We also covered creating and importing libraries, organizing larger projects with workspaces, and saw a **real-world example** of building a modular CLI application to manage user data. These tools and techniques will help you build well-organized, maintainable Rust applications. In the next chapter, we'll explore **testing** in Rust and how to ensure the correctness of your code with unit and integration tests.

CHAPTER 9

CONCURRENCY IN RUST

Concurrency is the ability to perform multiple tasks at the same time, and it's a critical feature for modern software. Rust's approach to concurrency ensures that you can write highly concurrent programs without the risk of data races or undefined behavior. In this chapter, we will explore Rust's approach to concurrency, including threads, the async/await pattern, mutexes, channels, and atomic operations. We'll conclude with a real-world example of building a **multi-threaded HTTP server**.

Understanding Rust's Approach to Concurrency

Rust's concurrency model is designed to prevent **data races**, which are common issues in multi-threaded programming. A **data race** occurs when multiple threads access the same piece of memory simultaneously, and at least one of them modifies the data. Rust prevents data races through its ownership and borrowing system, which guarantees that at any given time:

1. Data can either be accessed by **one mutable reference** or **many immutable references**, but not both.

2. The ownership of data can only be transferred once, and Rust ensures that references are not used after the data they refer to has been deallocated.

Rust achieves this safety without needing a garbage collector, making its concurrency model both **safe** and **efficient**.

Threads and the Async/Await Pattern

Rust provides two primary ways to handle concurrency: **threads** and the **async/await** pattern.

Threads:

Threads allow for parallel execution of code, where each thread runs concurrently and can execute different tasks. Rust provides the `std::thread` module to spawn and manage threads.

Example of spawning a thread:

```
rust
```

```
use std::thread;

fn main() {
    let handle = thread::spawn(|| {
        println!("Hello from the thread!");
    });

    // Wait for the thread to finish
    handle.join().unwrap();
}
```

In this example:

- We use `thread::spawn` to create a new thread that runs a closure.
- The `join()` method waits for the thread to finish its execution. If the thread panics, `unwrap()` will handle the error.

Async/Await Pattern:

The **async/await** pattern is used for asynchronous programming, allowing code to perform non-blocking operations. This is useful when dealing with I/O-bound tasks (e.g., reading from a file or making a network request) where you don't want to block other tasks while waiting for results.

In Rust, the `async` keyword is used to define an asynchronous function, and `await` is used to wait for the result of an asynchronous operation.

Example of async/await:

```rust
use tokio; // A popular async runtime

async fn say_hello() {
    println!("Hello, async world!");
}

#[tokio::main]
async fn main() {
    say_hello().await;
}
```

In this example:

- We define an asynchronous function `say_hello` with the `async` keyword.
- The `await` keyword is used to execute the asynchronous function, ensuring that we don't block the main thread.

Rust's async system is **zero-cost** and based on **futures**. Futures represent values that are computed asynchronously.

The async/await pattern allows you to write asynchronous code in a sequential style, making it easier to read and reason about.

Mutexes, Channels, and Atomic Operations

Rust provides several synchronization primitives to handle shared data between threads safely:

Mutexes:

A **mutex** (short for "mutual exclusion") is a synchronization primitive that allows only one thread to access a resource at a time. Rust's `std::sync::Mutex` is used to protect data that is shared across threads.

Example using a `Mutex`:

rust

```
use std::sync::{Arc, Mutex};
use std::thread;

fn main() {
    let counter = Arc::new(Mutex::new(0));
```

```
let mut handles = vec![];

for _ in 0..10 {
    let counter = Arc::clone(&counter);

    let handle = thread::spawn(move || {
        let mut num =
counter.lock().unwrap();
        *num += 1;
    });

    handles.push(handle);
}

for handle in handles {
    handle.join().unwrap();
}

println!("Counter:                    {}",
*counter.lock().unwrap());
}
```

In this example:

- We use Arc<Mutex<T>> to share ownership of the Mutex across multiple threads. Arc is an atomic reference counter that ensures the data is not deallocated while in use.

- The `lock()` method is used to access the data inside the `Mutex`. The lock ensures that only one thread can modify the data at a time.
- We increment the counter in each thread, ensuring safe concurrent access to the counter.

Channels:

Channels provide a way to send data between threads. A channel consists of a **sender** and a **receiver**, which are used to send and receive data respectively.

Example using a channel:

rust

```
use std::sync::mpsc;
use std::thread;

fn main() {
    let (tx, rx) = mpsc::channel();

    thread::spawn(move || {
        tx.send("Hello from thread").unwrap();
    });

    let message = rx.recv().unwrap();
    println!("{}", message);
```

```
}
```

In this example:

- We create a channel using `mpsc::channel()`, which returns a sender (`tx`) and a receiver (`rx`).
- A new thread is spawned, and the sender is used to send a message to the main thread.
- The receiver waits for a message and prints it when it arrives.

Atomic Operations:

Atomic operations allow for lock-free concurrency by ensuring that certain operations (e.g., incrementing a counter) are completed in a single, uninterrupted step.

Example using atomic operations:

rust

```rust
use std::sync::atomic::{AtomicUsize, Ordering};
use std::thread;

fn main() {
    let counter = AtomicUsize::new(0);

    let mut handles = vec![];
```

```rust
for _ in 0..10 {
        let counter = &counter;

        let handle = thread::spawn(move || {
            counter.fetch_add(1,
Ordering::SeqCst);
        });

        handles.push(handle);
    }

    for handle in handles {
        handle.join().unwrap();
    }

    println!("Counter:                    {}",
counter.load(Ordering::SeqCst));
}
```

In this example:

- We use `AtomicUsize` to represent a counter that can be safely accessed across threads without the need for locks.
- The `fetch_add()` method atomically increments the counter, and `load()` retrieves the current value.
- The `Ordering::SeqCst` argument ensures sequential consistency, meaning that the operations are completed in a predictable order.

Real-World Example: Building a Multi-threaded HTTP Server

Let's now apply our understanding of concurrency to build a **multi-threaded HTTP server**. The server will handle multiple incoming requests concurrently, using Rust's thread and networking features.

rust

```
use std::io::{Read, Write};
use std::net::{TcpListener, TcpStream};
use std::thread;

fn handle_client(mut stream: TcpStream) {
    let mut buffer = [0; 1024];
    stream.read(&mut buffer).unwrap();
    stream.write(b"HTTP/1.1 200 OK\r\nContent-
Length: 13\r\n\r\nHello, world!").unwrap();
}

fn main() {
    let listener =
TcpListener::bind("127.0.0.1:7878").unwrap();
    println!("Server running on
127.0.0.1:7878");

    for stream in listener.incoming() {
        match stream {
```

115

```
Ok(stream) => {
    thread::spawn(move || {
        handle_client(stream);
    });
}
Err(e) => {
    println!("Connection      failed:
{}", e);
        }
    }
  }
}
```

In this example:

- We use `TcpListener::bind` to create a TCP listener that listens for incoming connections on port 7878.
- For each incoming connection, a new thread is spawned using `thread::spawn`. This ensures that each client request is handled concurrently.
- The `handle_client` function reads the request from the client and sends a simple HTTP response.

Conclusion

In this chapter, we explored Rust's concurrency model, including how it uses threads, the async/await pattern, and synchronization primitives like mutexes, channels, and atomic operations to ensure safe and efficient concurrent programming. We also saw a real-world example of building a **multi-threaded HTTP server**, which demonstrates how to handle multiple requests simultaneously while ensuring thread safety. Rust's approach to concurrency makes it an excellent choice for writing high-performance, multi-threaded applications. In the next chapter, we'll explore **memory safety** in more depth, diving into how Rust ensures memory safety during concurrent operations.

CHAPTER 10

LIFETIMES AND BORROW CHECKER

In this chapter, we'll explore one of the most important features of Rust: **lifetimes**. Rust's borrow checker and lifetime system are critical to ensuring memory safety without needing a garbage collector. Understanding lifetimes and how the borrow checker works will help you write efficient, safe, and concurrent Rust code. We'll cover the role of lifetimes in memory safety, how the borrow checker prevents data races, advanced lifetime concepts, and conclude with a real-world example of managing **complex data structures**.

Understanding Lifetimes and Their Role in Memory Safety

A **lifetime** in Rust represents the scope of validity of a reference. Essentially, lifetimes tell Rust how long a reference to a piece of data is valid. This is important because it allows Rust to ensure that references never outlive the data they refer to, preventing **dangling references** — a common source of memory errors in many languages.

In Rust, every reference has a lifetime, and the Rust compiler tracks the relationship between the lifetimes of references and the data they refer to. Rust's lifetime system ensures that:

1. **References cannot outlive the data they point to.**
2. **Multiple references to the same data cannot cause data races.**
3. **References are not used after the data they point to has been dropped.**

Basic Lifetime Syntax:

In Rust, lifetimes are annotated using a ' symbol, followed by an identifier (e.g., 'a, 'b). When you define functions or structs that use references, you specify the lifetimes of those references to make sure they are valid for the correct duration.

Here's a simple example of a lifetime annotation in a function:

```rust
```

```
fn longest<'a>(s1: &'a str, s2: &'a str) -> &'a
str {
    if s1.len() > s2.len() {
        s1
    } else {
        s2
    }
}
```

In this function:

- The lifetime 'a ensures that both s1 and s2 must be valid for the same duration, and the function will return a reference that is valid for the same duration as the inputs.
- The function guarantees that the returned reference will not outlive either s1 or s2.

How the Borrow Checker Works to Prevent Data Races

Rust's **borrow checker** is responsible for ensuring that memory safety is maintained during both compile time and runtime. It enforces rules that guarantee that:

- **No mutable references coexist with immutable references.**
  This ensures that data cannot be modified while it's

being accessed by another part of the code, which prevents **data races**.

- **No references outlive the data they point to.** This prevents **dangling references**, where a reference might be used after the memory it points to has been freed.

Example of Borrowing with the Borrow Checker:

rust

```
fn main() {
    let s1 = String::from("Hello");
    let s2 = &s1;    // Immutable borrow
    let s3 = &s1;    // Immutable borrow
    // let s4 = &mut s1; // Error: cannot borrow
`s1` as mutable because it's already borrowed as
immutable
    println!("{}", s2);
}
```

In this example:

- s2 and s3 are immutable references to s1. Rust allows multiple immutable references because they do not change the data.
- Attempting to create a mutable reference (s4) while immutable references exist would result in a compile-time error. Rust enforces the rule that either **multiple**

121

immutable references or **one mutable reference** can exist at any time, but not both.

The borrow checker also ensures that when a reference is no longer needed, it can be safely dropped, and no other code can access that reference after its data has been deallocated.

Advanced Lifetime Concepts

While the basic lifetime system is straightforward, there are more advanced concepts that can help you write more complex and efficient code.

Lifetime Elision:

Rust's **lifetime elision** rules allow the compiler to infer lifetimes in simple cases, so you don't need to annotate them explicitly. For example, when defining functions, the compiler can automatically figure out the correct lifetimes if they follow certain patterns.

rust

```rust
fn first_word(s: &str) -> &str {
    s.split_whitespace().next().unwrap()
}
```

In this example, Rust infers that the lifetime of the return type is the same as the input string `s` because of the elision rules.

Static Lifetime:

The `'static` lifetime represents the entire duration of the program. It is used for data that is available for the entire runtime of the program, such as string literals.

rust

```
fn static_lifetime_example() -> &'static str {
    "This string has a 'static lifetime"
}
```

In this example, the returned string has a `'static` lifetime, meaning it exists for the entire program duration.

Lifetime Bounds on Structs:

When dealing with structs that contain references, you need to annotate lifetimes to ensure that the references are valid as long as the struct itself is valid.

rust

```
struct Book<'a> {
```

```
    title: &'a str,
    author: &'a str,
}


fn create_book<'a>(title: &'a str, author: &'a
str) -> Book<'a> {
    Book { title, author }
}
```

Here, the `Book` struct contains references with the lifetime `'a`, and the `create_book` function ensures that the references to `title` and `author` live long enough to be used in the struct.

Real-World Example: Managing Complex Data Structures

Let's apply what we've learned about lifetimes to a real-world example. We'll manage a complex data structure containing multiple references, such as a **library system** that keeps track of books and authors.

```
rust


struct Book<'a> {
    title: &'a str,
    author: &'a str,
```

```rust
}

struct Library<'a> {
    books: Vec<Book<'a>>,
}

impl<'a> Library<'a> {
    fn add_book(&mut self, title: &'a str,
author: &'a str) {
        let book = Book { title, author };
        self.books.push(book);
    }

    fn find_book_by_title(&self, title: &str) ->
Option<&Book<'a>> {
        self.books.iter().find(|&book|
book.title == title)
    }
}

fn main() {
    let author = String::from("J.K. Rowling");
    let book1 = String::from("Harry Potter and
the Sorcerer's Stone");
    let book2 = String::from("Harry Potter and
the Chamber of Secrets");

    let mut library = Library { books: Vec::new()
};
```

```
library.add_book(&book1, &author);
library.add_book(&book2, &author);

let                found_book                =
library.find_book_by_title("Harry Potter and the
Sorcerer's Stone");
    match found_book {
        Some(book) => println!("Found book: {} by
{}", book.title, book.author),
        None => println!("Book not found"),
    }
}
```

In this example:

- We define a `Book` struct that contains references to the title and author, with a lifetime `'a` to ensure these references are valid for as long as the `Book` is in use.
- We define a `Library` struct that contains a vector of `Book` objects, where the lifetime of each `Book` is tied to the lifetime of the `Library`.
- The `add_book` method adds a book to the library, and the `find_book_by_title` method searches for a book by its title.
- In the `main` function, we create string literals for the book titles and the author's name, ensuring they live long enough to be referenced by the `Book` struct.

Conclusion

In this chapter, we've covered the key concepts of **lifetimes** in Rust and how they play a crucial role in ensuring **memory safety**. We explored how the **borrow checker** prevents issues like data races and dangling references by enforcing lifetime rules. We also discussed **advanced lifetime concepts**, including lifetime elision, static lifetimes, and lifetime bounds on structs. Finally, we applied these concepts to a real-world example, managing complex data structures like a **library system** that tracks books and authors. Understanding lifetimes and how they interact with Rust's ownership and borrowing system will help you write safe, efficient, and scalable code. In the next chapter, we'll explore **error handling** in greater detail and discuss how to manage errors effectively in Rust programs.

CHAPTER 11

SMART POINTERS AND OWNERSHIP WITH RC AND ARC

In Rust, memory management is a key concern, especially when dealing with complex data structures and multiple references to the same data. While Rust's ownership model ensures memory safety without needing a garbage collector, **smart pointers** provide more flexibility when managing memory. In this chapter, we will explore **smart pointers** in Rust, including **Box**, **Rc**, and **Arc**. We'll cover how these pointers help with efficient memory management, reference counting, and shared ownership, especially across threads. Finally, we'll work through a **real-world example** of using shared ownership in a **GUI application**.

What are Smart Pointers in Rust?

A **smart pointer** is a data structure that acts like a pointer but also manages the memory it points to. In addition to providing basic functionality for handling memory (like regular pointers), smart pointers automatically handle tasks such as deallocation, reference counting, or memory sharing, which makes them safer and more convenient to use.

Rust's smart pointers include:

- **Box<T>**: A pointer for heap-allocated data.
- **Rc<T>**: A reference-counted pointer for single-threaded use.
- **Arc<T>**: An atomic reference-counted pointer for multi-threaded use.

These smart pointers help to manage ownership in different contexts, especially when you want to share data safely across parts of your program.

Using Box, Rc, and Arc for Efficient Memory Management

Let's take a closer look at the three primary smart pointers in Rust:

Box<T>:

Box<T> is used for **heap allocation**. It enables you to store data on the heap instead of the stack. The primary use case for Box is when you need a **single owner** of the data. Once the `Box` goes out of scope, the memory is automatically freed.

rust

```
fn main() {
    let b = Box::new(5); // Box allocates 5 on
the heap
    println!("Value in Box: {}", b);
}   // b goes out of scope and the memory is
deallocated
```

In this example, the integer 5 is allocated on the heap, and `Box` ensures that memory is properly cleaned up when the variable `b` goes out of scope.

Rc<T>:

Rc<T> stands for **Reference Counted** and is used when you want **shared ownership** of data, but **only within a single thread**. It tracks how many references there are to a piece of data, and when the reference count drops to zero, the memory is deallocated.

rust

```
use std::rc::Rc;
```

```rust
fn main() {
    let s = Rc::new(String::from("Hello, Rc!"));
    let t = Rc::clone(&s); // Cloning Rc creates
a new reference to the same data
    println!("String from Rc: {}", t);
} // s and t go out of scope, and memory is freed
```

Here, `Rc::new` creates a new reference-counted pointer. By calling `Rc::clone`, we create another reference to the same `String` on the heap. The data is only cleaned up once the reference count is zero.

Arc<T>:

Arc<T> (Atomic Reference Counted) is similar to Rc<T>, but it's thread-safe, making it useful when you need to share ownership of data across **multiple threads**. Arc<T> uses atomic operations to update the reference count, which ensures that the data is safely shared among threads.

```rust
rust

use std::sync::Arc;
use std::thread;

fn main() {
    let data = Arc::new(String::from("Shared
across threads"));
```

```
let data_clone = Arc::clone(&data);

thread::spawn(move || {
    println!("Thread 1: {}", data_clone);
});

println!("Main thread: {}", data);
}  // data is shared safely between threads
```

In this example, `Arc::clone` creates a new reference to the `String` in the heap, which is safely shared between the main thread and a spawned thread. `Arc` ensures that the reference count is handled atomically and safely across threads.

Reference Counting and Memory Sharing Across Threads

One of the core features of `Rc` and `Arc` is **reference counting**. Reference counting ensures that when multiple owners exist for a piece of data, the data is only deallocated when all owners are done using it. This is particularly useful when you need to share data among different parts of a program or across threads.

- **Rc<T>**: Suitable for single-threaded scenarios where multiple parts of the program need to access the same data.

- **Arc<T>**: Suitable for multi-threaded programs where data needs to be shared safely between threads.

When working with Rc or Arc, Rust ensures memory safety by ensuring that when the reference count reaches zero, the memory is cleaned up.

Example of Reference Counting with Rc<T>:

rust

```rust
use std::rc::Rc;

fn main() {
    let s1 = Rc::new(String::from("Rust is awesome!"));
    let s2 = Rc::clone(&s1);    // Increment reference count
    let s3 = Rc::clone(&s1);    // Increment reference count

    println!("Reference count: {}", Rc::strong_count(&s1));  // Prints: 3
}   // Memory is freed when the reference count drops to zero
```

In this example, we use Rc::strong_count to check the reference count, which will show 3 because there are three references to the `String`. Once all references go out of scope, the memory is deallocated.

Example of Memory Sharing with Arc<T> Across Threads:
rust

```
use std::sync::Arc;
use std::thread;

fn main() {
    let data = Arc::new(vec![1, 2, 3, 4, 5]);

    let mut handles = vec![];

    for _ in 0..5 {
        let data_clone = Arc::clone(&data);

        let handle = thread::spawn(move || {
            println!("{:?}", data_clone);
        });

        handles.push(handle);
    }

    for handle in handles {
        handle.join().unwrap();
    }
}
```

In this example, `Arc` allows multiple threads to share access to the `Vec` safely. Each thread gets a reference to the same data, and once all threads finish executing, the memory is freed.

Real-World Example: Shared Ownership in GUI Applications

In many GUI applications, multiple parts of the application (e.g., buttons, text fields, and event handlers) need to access and modify shared data. Using smart pointers like `Rc` or `Arc` allows you to share ownership of data safely. Let's build a simple example using `Rc` to manage shared ownership of a **GUI component**.

Example: A Simple GUI Application with Shared Ownership

rust

```rust
use std::rc::Rc;
use std::cell::RefCell;

#[derive(Debug)]
struct Button {
    label: String,
    click_count: Rc<RefCell<i32>>,
}
```

```rust
impl Button {
    fn new(label: &str) -> Button {
        Button {
            label: label.to_string(),
            click_count:
Rc::new(RefCell::new(0)),
        }
    }

    fn click(&self) {
        let         mut         count         =
self.click_count.borrow_mut();
        *count += 1;
        println!("Button '{}' clicked {} times",
self.label, *count);
    }
}

fn main() {
    let button = Button::new("Submit");

    let             button_clone             =
Rc::clone(&button.click_count);      //     Share
ownership of the click count

    button.click();  // First click
    button.click();  // Second click
```

```
    // Simulating another part of the program
accessing the click count
    button_clone.borrow_mut();          //     The
`button_clone` allows access to the click count
    button.click();  // Third click
}
```

In this example:

- We define a `Button` struct that has a `label` and a `click_count` field.
- The `click_count` is wrapped in a `RefCell` and an `Rc` to allow shared ownership and **mutable** borrowing. `RefCell` enables interior mutability, which means we can mutate the `click_count` even if the `Button` struct itself is immutable.
- Each time the button is clicked, the `click` method increments the `click_count`.

The use of `Rc` allows multiple parts of the application to share ownership of the button's state (`click_count`). The `RefCell` is used to allow interior mutability, letting us modify the `click_count` while maintaining the overall immutability of the `Button` object.

Conclusion

In this chapter, we explored **smart pointers** in Rust, including **Box**, **Rc**, and **Arc**, which are used to manage memory efficiently and safely. These smart pointers offer different types of memory management:

- `Box<T>` for heap allocation and single ownership.
- `Rc<T>` for shared ownership in single-threaded contexts.
- `Arc<T>` for thread-safe shared ownership across threads.

We also covered **reference counting** and how it allows for **memory sharing** safely across threads, as well as **real-world examples** where shared ownership is particularly useful, such as in **GUI applications**.

Rust's approach to memory management, combined with smart pointers and its ownership model, enables developers to write safe and efficient programs without worrying about memory leaks or dangling references. In the next chapter, we'll explore **advanced concurrency techniques** and how Rust's concurrency model can be leveraged for building scalable applications.

CHAPTER 12

MACROS IN RUST

In Rust, **macros** are a powerful tool that can reduce boilerplate code, improve efficiency, and allow you to write more expressive and flexible code. Macros in Rust are similar to functions, but they operate on the **syntax level** rather than the **value level**. This chapter will explore how to define and use macros in Rust, explain `macro_rules!`, and provide real-world examples of how macros can be used to reduce boilerplate code. We'll finish with a practical example of creating a **custom logging system** using macros.

Defining and Using Macros

A **macro** in Rust is a way of writing code that writes other code. Macros can generate code at compile time based on patterns, making them incredibly useful in situations where you need repetitive code generation.

Basic Macro Example:

Rust provides two types of macros: **Declarative Macros** (using `macro_rules!`) and **Procedural Macros**. We'll focus on declarative macros for this chapter.

Here's an example of defining a basic macro using `macro_rules!`:

rust

```
macro_rules! say_hello {
    () => {
        println!("Hello, world!");
    };
}

fn main() {
    say_hello!();  // Invoking the macro
}
```

In this example:

- The macro `say_hello` takes no arguments and prints `"Hello, world!"` to the console.
- The macro is invoked using `say_hello!()`.

Macros can take arguments and generate code dynamically based on those arguments, making them more flexible.

Macro with Arguments:

Here's an example of a macro that takes arguments and uses them in its generated code:

rust

```
macro_rules! print_sum {
    ($a:expr, $b:expr) => {
        println!("The sum is: {}", $a + $b);
    };
}

fn main() {
    print_sum!(5, 10);  // Output: The sum is: 15
}
```

In this example, the macro `print_sum` takes two expressions (`$a` and `$b`) and prints their sum. When we call `print_sum!(5, 10)`, the macro expands into `println!("The sum is: {}", 5 + 10);`.

141

Understanding Rust's `macro_rules!`

Rust uses `macro_rules!` to define declarative macros. These macros allow you to specify patterns of input and the code that should be generated for that pattern. The basic syntax of `macro_rules!` is as follows:

rust

```
macro_rules! <macro_name> {
    (<pattern>) => {
        <code>;
    };
}
```

The **pattern** is the input the macro matches, and the **code** is the output generated when the macro is invoked. Patterns are typically specified using **Rust's syntax** (e.g., variables, expressions, blocks) and **metavariables** (like `$a:expr` for expressions).

Macro Patterns and Matching:

Here's a more complex example where the macro matches different patterns:

rust

```
macro_rules! add {
    ($x:expr, $y:expr) => {
        $x + $y
    };
    ($x:expr, $y:expr, $z:expr) => {
        $x + $y + $z
    };
}

fn main() {
    println!("Sum of two numbers: {}", add!(2,
3));  // Output: 5
    println!("Sum of three numbers: {}", add!(2,
3, 4));  // Output: 9
}
```

This macro matches two different patterns:

1. When it's given two arguments, it returns their sum.
2. When it's given three arguments, it sums all three.

By defining different patterns, the macro can be customized for various use cases, reducing repetitive code.

Use Cases for Macros in Reducing Boilerplate Code

One of the most common use cases for macros is to reduce **boilerplate code**. Boilerplate refers to repetitive code that doesn't add much value but is necessary to make the program work. Macros help eliminate the need for writing the same code repeatedly by generating it at compile time.

Here are a few areas where macros are particularly useful:

1. Code Generation for Repetitive Tasks:

Macros are ideal for generating repetitive code, such as implementing common methods for multiple structs or generating similar logic for many places in your program.

For example, let's say you have several structs that need to implement a `to_string` method. Instead of writing the same method for each struct, you can define a macro:

rust

```
macro_rules! to_string_impl {
    ($struct_name:ident) => {
        impl $struct_name {
            fn to_string(&self) -> String {
                format!("{:?}", self)
            }
```

144

```
            }
        };
    }

    struct Person {
        name: String,
        age: u32,
    }

    to_string_impl!(Person);

    fn main() {
        let person = Person {
            name: String::from("Alice"),
            age: 30,
        };
        println!("{}", person.to_string());        //
    Output: Person { name: "Alice", age: 30 }
    }
```

The `to_string_impl!` macro generates the `to_string` method for any struct you specify, which reduces repetitive code.

2. Simplifying Conditional Logic or Matching:

Macros can help simplify complex conditional logic or pattern matching. For example, consider handling different levels of logging messages (info, warning, error):

rust

```rust
macro_rules! log {
    (info, $message:expr) => {
        println!("[INFO]: {}", $message);
    };
    (warning, $message:expr) => {
        println!("[WARNING]: {}", $message);
    };
    (error, $message:expr) => {
        println!("[ERROR]: {}", $message);
    };
}

fn main() {
    log!(info,    "This    is    an    informational
message");
    log!(warning, "This is a warning");
    log!(error, "This is an error message");
}
```

In this case, the macro log! reduces the need for repeated if or match statements for different types of logging. Instead, you can call the macro with the appropriate log level (info, warning, or error), which makes the code more concise and readable.

Real-World Example: Custom Logging System with Macros

Let's create a simple **custom logging system** using macros to handle different levels of logging (e.g., INFO, ERROR, DEBUG) efficiently.

Creating the Logging Macro System:

rust

```rust
macro_rules! log_info {
    ($message:expr) => {
        println!("[INFO] {}", $message);
    };
}

macro_rules! log_error {
    ($message:expr) => {
        println!("[ERROR] {}", $message);
    };
}

macro_rules! log_debug {
    ($message:expr) => {
        println!("[DEBUG] {}", $message);
    };
}

fn main() {
    let user_input = "Hello, world!";
```

147

```
    log_info!("User    input    received:    {}",
user_input);

    let error_message = "File not found";
    log_error!("Error: {}", error_message);

    log_debug!("Debugging    the    user    input
processing logic.");
}
```

Explanation:

- We define three macros: `log_info!`, `log_error!`, and `log_debug!`. Each macro takes a message expression and prints it with the appropriate log level (INFO, ERROR, or DEBUG).

- These macros allow us to easily generate log messages without needing to repeat the formatting logic each time we log something.

Output:

pgsql

```
[INFO] User input received: Hello, world!
[ERROR] Error: File not found
[DEBUG] Debugging    the    user    input    processing
logic.
```

In this case, the macros significantly reduce the need for boilerplate code for logging and provide a concise way to handle different log levels. You can easily expand this to support additional log levels, output formatting, or even write to a file instead of printing to the console.

Conclusion

In this chapter, we've explored how **macros** in Rust help reduce boilerplate code by generating repetitive tasks and simplifying complex patterns. We defined basic macros and saw how Rust's `macro_rules!` allows you to create powerful, flexible macros for code generation. We also explored real-world use cases, such as logging and reducing repetitive code in complex data structures. The custom logging system example showed how macros can streamline common tasks and make your Rust code more readable and maintainable.

In the next chapter, we'll look at **error handling** in Rust and discuss how to effectively manage errors and exceptions in your programs using Rust's `Result` and `Option` types.

CHAPTER 13

ASYNCHRONOUS PROGRAMMING IN RUST

Asynchronous programming allows you to write programs that can perform tasks concurrently without blocking the main thread, making it especially useful for I/O-bound tasks such as network requests, file reading, or waiting for user input. Rust provides a robust model for asynchronous programming with the **async/await** syntax, which enables efficient, non-blocking operations. In this chapter, we'll explore the async/await model, how to work with `Future` and `Stream`, implement asynchronous I/O operations, and walk through a real-world example of building an **asynchronous web scraper**.

Understanding the Async/Await Model

Rust's **async/await** model is built on **futures**, which are values that represent a value that is not yet available but will be computed asynchronously. When using `async` and `await`, Rust allows you to write asynchronous code that looks and behaves similarly to synchronous code, making it easier to understand and maintain.

The `async` Keyword:

The `async` keyword is used to define a function or block of code that returns a **future**. When you mark a function as `async`, it automatically returns a `Future` that you can `.await` to get the result.

rust

```rust
async fn say_hello() {
    println!("Hello, async world!");
}

fn main() {
    let future = say_hello();  // This returns a Future
    // To execute the async code, we need an
    executor (e.g., tokio or async-std)
}
```

In this example, the `say_hello` function is marked as `async`, and it returns a future. To actually run the function, we need an asynchronous runtime (such as `tokio` or `async-std`) to execute the future.

The `await` Keyword:

The `await` keyword is used to **wait** for a future to resolve and get its value. When you use `await`, the function will pause at that point and yield control until the future has been completed, allowing other tasks to run concurrently.

rust

```rust
async fn say_hello() {
    println!("Hello, async world!");
}

#[tokio::main]
async fn main() {
    say_hello().await;   // Await the result of
the async function
}
```

Here, `say_hello().await` tells the program to wait for `say_hello` to finish executing before continuing.

Working with Future and Stream

In Rust, two primary traits are central to asynchronous programming: **Future** and **Stream**.

The Future Trait:

A **future** represents a value that may not be available yet but will be eventually. The Future trait provides the .poll() method to check if the future is ready.

You can think of a Future as a placeholder for a result that will be computed asynchronously. The await keyword simplifies working with futures by handling polling and waiting for completion.

```rust
use std::future::Future;

async fn foo() -> i32 {
    42
}

fn main() {
    let future = foo(); // `future` is a
Future<i32>
    let result =
futures::executor::block_on(future); // Blocking
to get the result
    println!("The result is: {}", result);
}
```

In this example, `foo()` returns a `Future<i32>`, and we use `block_on()` to wait for it to resolve, effectively blocking the main thread until the future is complete.

The `Stream` Trait:

A **stream** is similar to a `Future`, but instead of representing a single value, it represents a series of values that are yielded over time (like an asynchronous iterator). The `Stream` trait provides a `.next()` method that returns a `Future<Option<T>>`, where `T` is the type of value produced by the stream.

rust

```
use futures::stream;
use futures::StreamExt;

async fn count_up_to(n: u32) -> impl Stream<Item
= u32> {
    stream::iter(1..=n)
}

#[tokio::main]
async fn main() {
    let mut stream = count_up_to(5);
    while let Some(val) = stream.next().await {
        println!("{}", val);
```

```
    }
}
```

In this example:

- `count_up_to` returns a stream of numbers from 1 to `n`.
- We use `stream.next().await` to consume each item in the stream asynchronously.

Implementing Asynchronous I/O Operations

Asynchronous programming is especially useful for I/O-bound tasks such as reading files, making network requests, or handling multiple client connections in a server. Rust's async ecosystem is built around **async runtimes** such as **Tokio** and **async-std**, which provide tools to perform asynchronous I/O operations.

Example: Asynchronous File Reading (Using `tokio`)

Here's an example of reading a file asynchronously using the `tokio` runtime:

```rust
use tokio::fs::File;
use tokio::io::{self, AsyncReadExt};
```

```rust
#[tokio::main]
async fn main() -> io::Result<()> {
    let                mut                file            =
File::open("example.txt").await?;
    let mut contents = vec![];

    file.read_to_end(&mut contents).await?;

    println!("File            content:              {}",
String::from_utf8_lossy(&contents));
    Ok(())
}
```

In this example:

- We use `tokio::fs::File` to open the file asynchronously.
- The `read_to_end` method reads the entire file asynchronously and stores it in the `contents` vector.
- `await` is used to wait for the asynchronous operations to complete.

Handling Multiple Asynchronous Tasks:

Rust's async model allows you to run multiple tasks concurrently, which is helpful when you need to perform several I/O-bound tasks simultaneously.

```rust
rust

use tokio::task;

#[tokio::main]
async fn main() {
    let task1 = task::spawn(async {
        // Simulate some async work
        println!("Task 1 is running");
    });

    let task2 = task::spawn(async {
        // Simulate some async work
        println!("Task 2 is running");
    });

    // Wait for both tasks to finish
    let _ = tokio::try_join!(task1, task2);
}
```

In this example:

- We spawn two asynchronous tasks concurrently using `task::spawn`.
- `tokio::try_join!` is used to wait for both tasks to complete.

Real-World Example: Building an Asynchronous Web Scraper

Let's use what we've learned about asynchronous programming to build a simple **web scraper**. The scraper will make asynchronous HTTP requests to fetch web pages and extract some data from them.

We'll use the `reqwest` crate for making HTTP requests and `tokio` for managing the async runtime.

Step 1: Add Dependencies

In `Cargo.toml`, add the dependencies for `reqwest` and `tokio`:

toml

```
[dependencies]
tokio = { version = "1", features = ["full"] }
reqwest = "0.11"
```

Step 2: Write the Web Scraper

Here's the code for the web scraper:

rust

```
use reqwest::Error;
```

```
#[tokio::main]
async fn main() -> Result<(), Error> {
    let urls = vec![
        "https://www.rust-lang.org",
        "https://www.github.com",
        "https://www.reddit.com",
    ];

    let mut handles = vec![];

    for url in urls {
        let handle = tokio::spawn(async move {
            let body = reqwest::get(url)
                .await
                .expect("Failed    to    send request")
                .text()
                .await
                .expect("Failed to read response text");

            println!("Fetched  {}:  {}  bytes", url, body.len());
        });

        handles.push(handle);
    }

    // Wait for all tasks to complete
```

```
for handle in handles {
    handle.await.unwrap();
}


Ok(())
}
```

Explanation:

- We create a vector of URLs that we want to scrape.
- For each URL, we use `tokio::spawn` to create a new asynchronous task that fetches the page content using `reqwest::get`.
- We collect the handles for all tasks and wait for them to finish using `.await`.

Output:

nginx

```
Fetched https://www.rust-lang.org: 12345 bytes
Fetched https://www.github.com: 98765 bytes
Fetched https://www.reddit.com: 43210 bytes
```

In this example, the scraper performs **three asynchronous HTTP requests** concurrently, waiting for each response without blocking other requests. This allows the program to scrape multiple web pages at once, improving efficiency.

Conclusion

In this chapter, we've explored **asynchronous programming** in Rust using the `async/await` model. We discussed:

- How to use `async` and `await` for writing asynchronous code.
- Working with the `Future` and `Stream` traits for asynchronous computations.
- Implementing asynchronous I/O operations using runtimes like `tokio`.
- A real-world example of building an **asynchronous web scraper** that makes concurrent HTTP requests.

Asynchronous programming in Rust is a powerful tool that allows you to write efficient, non-blocking code, especially for I/O-bound tasks. In the next chapter, we'll explore **error handling** in greater detail and discuss how to manage errors effectively in Rust applications.

CHAPTER 14

TESTING AND DEBUGGING IN RUST

Testing and debugging are essential components of the software development process, ensuring that your code is correct, efficient, and free from bugs. Rust provides a powerful testing framework that makes it easy to write **unit tests** and **integration tests**. Additionally, Rust has excellent debugging support with tools like **gdb** and **lldb**. In this chapter, we'll cover how to write tests in Rust, debug code, and safely test concurrent code. We'll conclude with a real-world example of building and testing a **math library**.

Writing Unit Tests and Integration Tests

Rust's built-in testing framework makes it easy to write and run both **unit tests** and **integration tests**. Unit tests allow you to verify the correctness of individual functions, while integration tests allow you to test multiple components working together.

162

Unit Tests:

Unit tests in Rust are written inside the `#[cfg(test)]` module. These tests are typically placed within the same file as the code they are testing.

Here's an example of writing unit tests for a simple function that adds two numbers:

rust

```
fn add(a: i32, b: i32) -> i32 {
    a + b
}

#[cfg(test)]
mod tests {
    use super::*;

    #[test]
    fn test_add_positive_numbers() {
        assert_eq!(add(2, 3), 5);
    }

    #[test]
    fn test_add_negative_numbers() {
        assert_eq!(add(-2, -3), -5);
    }
```

```
#[test]
fn test_add_mixed_numbers() {
    assert_eq!(add(-2, 3), 1);
}
}
```

In this example:

- The `add` function is tested with different scenarios: adding positive numbers, negative numbers, and a mix of both.
- The `#[cfg(test)]` attribute ensures that the test module is only compiled and run when testing.

Integration Tests:

Integration tests are typically placed in the `tests` directory (outside of the `src` directory) and are used to test the interaction between different modules.

Here's an example of an integration test:

1. Create a `tests` folder in your project root and create a file named `math_tests.rs` inside it.

rust

```
// In `tests/math_tests.rs`
```

```
use my_project::add; // Assuming `add` is public
in `my_project`

#[test]
fn test_addition() {
    assert_eq!(add(4, 5), 9);
}
```

In this example:

- We're testing the add function in an integration test, which is placed in a separate file.
- The #[test] attribute is used to mark a function as a test, and it is run with the rest of the tests when executed.

Running Tests:

To run tests in Rust, use the cargo test command:

```
bash
```

```
cargo test
```

This command will compile the tests and run them, showing the results in the terminal.

Debugging Rust Code with Tools like GDB and LLDB

Rust provides excellent support for debugging code using standard debuggers like **gdb** and **lldb**. These tools allow you to step through your code, inspect variables, and set breakpoints to help diagnose and fix issues.

Debugging with GDB and LLDB:

1. **Install GDB or LLDB:** If you don't have gdb or lldb installed, you can install them using your package manager (e.g., `apt-get`, `brew`).

2. **Building for Debugging:** By default, Rust compiles code in **release mode**, which optimizes for performance. For debugging, you should build the code in **debug mode**, which disables optimizations.

bash

```
cargo build
```

3. **Debugging with GDB:**

   You can start debugging your program with GDB by running:

   bash

```
gdb target/debug/my_project
```

Once inside GDB, you can set breakpoints, run the program, and inspect variables:

- o Set a breakpoint: `break main`
- o Start running the program: `run`
- o Inspect variables: `print my_variable`

4. **Debugging with LLDB:**

LLDB is another popular debugger that you can use with Rust. To start a debug session with LLDB:

```
bash
```

```
lldb target/debug/my_project
```

Inside LLDB, the commands are similar to GDB for setting breakpoints and inspecting values.

How to Test Concurrent Code Safely

Testing concurrent code can be challenging because multiple threads may be accessing shared data, leading to race conditions or other issues. Fortunately, Rust's ownership model and its synchronization primitives, like **Mutex** and **Arc**, make concurrent code easier to manage and test safely.

Testing Concurrent Code with Mutexes and Channels:

When testing concurrent code, you can use synchronization mechanisms like **Mutexes** or **Channels** to control access to shared data and ensure that the code behaves as expected.

Here's an example of testing a concurrent counter using **Mutex** and **Arc**:

rust

```
use std::sync::{Arc, Mutex};
use std::thread;

#[cfg(test)]
mod tests {
    use super::*;

    #[test]
    fn test_concurrent_counter() {
        let counter = Arc::new(Mutex::new(0));
        let mut handles = vec![];

        for _ in 0..10 {
            let counter = Arc::clone(&counter);
```

```rust
    let handle = thread::spawn(move || {
        let        mut        num        =
counter.lock().unwrap();
            *num += 1;
    });
    handles.push(handle);
}

for handle in handles {
    handle.join().unwrap();
}

let result = *counter.lock().unwrap();
assert_eq!(result, 10);
    }
}
```

In this example:

- We create a shared counter protected by a `Mutex`, wrapped in an `Arc` to allow shared ownership across multiple threads.
- Each thread increments the counter. After all threads finish, we check that the counter is `10`, ensuring that the threads correctly modified the shared data.

Running the Test:

You can run this concurrent test just like any other:

```bash
bash
```

```bash
cargo test
```

Rust's **ownership system** and synchronization primitives (like `Mutex` and `Arc`) ensure that even when dealing with concurrent code, you can safely manage access to shared data and write effective tests.

Real-World Example: Implementing and Testing a Math Library

Let's implement and test a simple math library that includes functions for addition, subtraction, multiplication, and division. This example will demonstrate both unit and integration tests.

Math Library Implementation:

Create a `math` module:

```rust
rust

// src/math.rs

pub fn add(a: i32, b: i32) -> i32 {
    a + b
```

```rust
}

pub fn subtract(a: i32, b: i32) -> i32 {
    a - b
}

pub fn multiply(a: i32, b: i32) -> i32 {
    a * b
}

pub fn divide(a: i32, b: i32) -> Result<i32, String> {
    if b == 0 {
        Err(String::from("Cannot divide by zero"))
    } else {
        Ok(a / b)
    }
}
```

Unit Tests for Math Library:

Add unit tests inside the `math` module:

rust

```
// src/math.rs

#[cfg(test)]
mod tests {
```

```rust
use super::*;

#[test]
fn test_add() {
    assert_eq!(add(2, 3), 5);
}

#[test]
fn test_subtract() {
    assert_eq!(subtract(5, 3), 2);
}

#[test]
fn test_multiply() {
    assert_eq!(multiply(3, 4), 12);
}

#[test]
fn test_divide() {
    assert_eq!(divide(6, 2), Ok(3));
    assert_eq!(divide(1,               0),
Err(String::from("Cannot divide by zero")));
    }
}
```

Integration Test:

Create a separate `tests` folder for integration tests. Add a file `math_tests.rs` to test the `math` library:

172

```rust

// tests/math_tests.rs

use my_project::math;  // Assuming math module is
public

#[test]
fn test_addition() {
    assert_eq!(math::add(4, 5), 9);
}

#[test]
fn test_subtraction() {
    assert_eq!(math::subtract(9, 5), 4);
}

#[test]
fn test_multiplication() {
    assert_eq!(math::multiply(3, 5), 15);
}

#[test]
fn test_division() {
    assert_eq!(math::divide(10, 2), Ok(5));
    assert_eq!(math::divide(5,                0),
Err(String::from("Cannot divide by zero")));
}
```

Running the Tests:

To run the tests, use:

```bash

cargo test
```

This will run both the unit tests and the integration tests, providing feedback on the correctness of your math library.

Conclusion

In this chapter, we explored how to **test and debug** Rust code, focusing on **unit tests**, **integration tests**, and **concurrent code testing**. We also looked at debugging with tools like **gdb** and **lldb**. We implemented a **math library** and wrote both unit and integration tests to ensure its correctness. Testing and debugging are crucial steps in ensuring that your code is reliable and efficient, and Rust's powerful tools make this process straightforward and effective. In the next chapter, we'll explore **memory management** in more detail, discussing smart pointers, ownership, and borrowing in Rust.

CHAPTER 15

PERFORMANCE OPTIMIZATION IN RUST

Rust is known for its high performance and low-level control over system resources, making it ideal for systems programming, high-performance applications, and cases where memory management is critical. In this chapter, we'll explore how to optimize Rust code for **better performance**. We'll cover Rust's **performance characteristics**, strategies for **optimizing memory usage and reducing allocations**, tools for **profiling and benchmarking**, and a **real-world example** of optimizing a database-backed application.

Understanding Rust's Performance Characteristics

Rust is designed to be **fast and efficient** while maintaining memory safety and concurrency guarantees. Its **performance characteristics** come from several key features:

1. **Zero-cost abstractions**: Rust's abstractions (like iterators, closures, and async) are designed to have zero overhead. This means you can use high-level features without sacrificing performance, as Rust will compile them down to efficient machine code.

2. **Manual memory management**: Rust gives you control over memory through its ownership system, but it also enforces safety rules to prevent issues like memory leaks, dangling pointers, and race conditions. This allows you to manage memory efficiently without relying on a garbage collector.

3. **No runtime**: Unlike languages with garbage collection or virtual machines, Rust doesn't have a runtime system that requires overhead. This means that Rust code typically has lower latency and uses fewer resources compared to other high-level languages.

4. **Efficient concurrency**: Rust's concurrency model ensures that concurrent code runs safely without requiring expensive synchronization primitives like mutexes and locks in many cases. This leads to lower contention and higher throughput in multi-threaded programs.

Optimizing Memory Usage and Reducing Allocations

Rust's performance is heavily influenced by how memory is allocated and managed. By reducing unnecessary memory allocations and being mindful of how data is stored and accessed, you can significantly improve performance.

1. Use Stack Allocation When Possible:

Rust's **stack allocation** is much faster than heap allocation. Therefore, it's important to use stack-allocated data when possible, rather than relying on heap-allocated structures like `Vec` or `String`.

rust

```
fn example() {
    let a = 5; // Stack-allocated
    let b = 10; // Stack-allocated
    let sum = a + b; // Fast computation on the
stack
}
```

In contrast, heap-allocated data structures like `Vec` or `String` require more overhead, as they involve dynamic memory allocation and deallocation.

2. Minimize Unnecessary Allocations:

Allocating memory can be expensive, especially if done frequently. In Rust, you can reduce unnecessary allocations by:

- Using **&str** instead of String when you don't need to mutate or own the string.
- Using **Vec::with_capacity()** to allocate a Vec with an initial capacity, avoiding multiple reallocations as the vector grows.

```rust
fn process_data(data: &[u8]) {
    let mut buffer = Vec::with_capacity(data.len()); // Pre-allocate memory
    for byte in data {
        buffer.push(*byte);
    }
}
```

This way, you reduce the number of reallocations and ensure more efficient memory usage.

3. Use Types When Appropriate:

Types like `i32`, `f64`, and other simple types implement the trait in Rust, meaning they can be **duplicated** efficiently without allocating new memory. If you work with small types like numbers or simple structures, prefer ing them over borrowing them if you need them in multiple places.

rust

```rust
fn main() {
    let x = 10;
    let y = x; // `x` is copied, no heap allocation
    println!("x: {}, y: {}", x, y);
}
```

This avoids the overhead of borrowing or reference counting.

4. Avoid Cloning Large Objects:

Calling `.clone()` on large data structures like `Vec` or `String` can result in unnecessary heap allocations and operations. Instead, use references or avoid cloning by restructuring your code to pass ownership.

rust

```
fn process_large_data(data: &Vec<i32>) {
    // Avoid cloning; pass a reference instead
    let result = data.iter().sum::<i32>();
    println!("Sum: {}", result);
}
```

Here, passing a reference (`&Vec<i32>`) prevents a costly clone operation.

Profiling and Benchmarking Tools

To effectively optimize code, it's essential to measure performance using profiling and benchmarking tools. These tools provide insights into where bottlenecks are occurring and which parts of the code need optimization.

1. `cargo bench` for Benchmarking:

Rust provides an integrated benchmarking tool through `cargo bench`. It uses the **criterion.rs** library to provide detailed statistics and benchmarking results.

To benchmark code in Rust, create a `benches` directory in your project and write a benchmark function:

```rust
rust

// In `benches/bench.rs`
use criterion::{black_box, Criterion};

fn bench_addition(c: &mut Criterion) {
    c.bench_function("add 2 + 2", |b| b.iter(||
2 + 2));
}

criterion_group!(benches, bench_addition);
criterion_main!(benches);
```

Run the benchmark with the following command:

```bash
bash

cargo bench
```

This will provide you with detailed information on the time it takes to perform the benchmarked operation, which is helpful for performance analysis.

2. `perf` and `gprof` for Profiling:

For deeper performance analysis, you can use external profiling tools such as `perf` (on Linux) or `gprof` to collect detailed performance data.

- **perf**: A Linux tool that can profile Rust programs and generate detailed reports on CPU usage, function call frequency, and more.

```bash

cargo build --release
perf record ./target/release/my_project
perf report
```

This will give you an in-depth analysis of where the program spends most of its time.

- **gprof**: A profiling tool that can generate a performance report based on function calls. It is particularly useful for identifying hotspots in your code.

3. `flamegraph` for Visual Profiling:

Flamegraphs provide a visual representation of performance data. They show which functions consume the most time, helping you easily identify bottlenecks.

To generate a flamegraph:

```bash

cargo install flamegraph
```

```
cargo flamegraph
```

This will generate a flamegraph of your Rust program, helping you pinpoint performance issues.

Real-World Example: Optimizing a Database-Backed Application

Let's apply what we've learned by optimizing a simple **database-backed application**. Assume we have an application that retrieves records from a database and performs some computational tasks on the data.

Initial Code (Without Optimization):
rust

```
use std::time::Instant;

fn fetch_records_from_db() -> Vec<i32> {
    // Simulate database retrieval
    (1..100_000).collect()
}

fn process_data(data: Vec<i32>) -> i32 {
    data.iter().map(|&x| x * 2).sum()
}

fn main() {
```

```
    let start = Instant::now();

    let data = fetch_records_from_db();
    let result = process_data(data);

    println!("Processed result: {}", result);
    println!("Elapsed        time:        {:?}",
start.elapsed());
}
```

Optimization 1: Avoid Cloning and Redundant Memory Allocations

The `fetch_records_from_db()` function returns a `Vec<i32>`, and `process_data()` takes ownership of this vector. If we don't need ownership in `process_data()`, we can pass a reference instead to avoid unnecessary memory allocations.

rust

```
fn process_data(data: &[i32]) -> i32 {
    data.iter().map(|&x| x * 2).sum()
}

fn main() {
    let start = Instant::now();

    let data = fetch_records_from_db();
```

```
let result = process_data(&data);  // Pass a
reference instead of cloning

    println!("Processed result: {}", result);
    println!("Elapsed         time:          {:?}",
start.elapsed());
}
```

Optimization 2: Parallelize Computations

We can also parallelize the `process_data` function using **Rayon**, a crate that simplifies data parallelism.

Add `rayon` to your `Cargo.toml`:

toml

```
[dependencies]
rayon = "1.5"
```

Modify `process_data()` to use Rayon for parallel processing:

rust

```
use rayon::prelude::*;

fn process_data(data: &[i32]) -> i32 {
    data.par_iter().map(|&x| x * 2).sum()
}
```

With `rayon::par_iter()`, the computation will be distributed across multiple threads, significantly improving performance for large datasets.

Final Optimized Code:

rust

```
use std::time::Instant;
use rayon::prelude::*;

fn fetch_records_from_db() -> Vec<i32> {
    (1..100_000).collect()
}

fn process_data(data: &[i32]) -> i32 {
    data.par_iter().map(|&x| x * 2).sum()
}

fn main() {
    let start = Instant::now();

    let data = fetch_records_from_db();
    let result = process_data(&data);

    println!("Processed result: {}", result);
    println!("Elapsed       time:       {:?}",
start.elapsed());
}
```

Now, the application performs parallel computation, reducing processing time significantly.

Conclusion

In this chapter, we explored **performance optimization** in Rust, focusing on the following:

- Understanding Rust's performance characteristics, such as zero-cost abstractions and manual memory management.
- Strategies for optimizing memory usage, including using stack allocation, minimizing allocations, and avoiding cloning large objects.
- Tools for profiling and benchmarking, such as `cargo bench`, `perf`, `gprof`, and `flamegraph`.
- A real-world example of optimizing a **database-backed application** by avoiding unnecessary memory allocations, parallelizing computations, and improving overall performance.

Rust's emphasis on performance, combined with its safety guarantees, makes it an excellent choice for high-performance applications. In the next chapter, we'll explore

advanced concurrency in Rust, focusing on building scalable, concurrent applications.

CHAPTER 16

RUST IN WEB DEVELOPMENT

Rust is increasingly being used for **web development** due to its **performance**, **safety**, and **concurrency** features. Rust's strong type system and memory safety guarantees make it a great choice for building fast and reliable web applications. In this chapter, we will explore how to get started with web development using Rust. We'll dive into using popular frameworks like **Rocket** and **Actix**, building and deploying a simple **REST API**, and create a real-world example of a web application that handles **real-time data**.

Introduction to Web Development with Rust

Web development in Rust is growing rapidly, with several frameworks available to build robust and efficient web applications. Rust provides a great alternative to languages like JavaScript, Python, and Ruby for backend development, especially for applications that require high performance or handle large amounts of concurrent requests.

Rust's web development ecosystem is still maturing, but with the help of popular libraries and frameworks like **Rocket**, **Actix**, and **Warp**, you can build and deploy web applications in Rust effectively.

Using Frameworks Like Rocket and Actix

Rust has several web frameworks, each with unique features and strengths. Let's explore **Rocket** and **Actix**, two of the most popular frameworks for building web applications in Rust.

Rocket:

Rocket is one of the most popular Rust frameworks, known for its **ease of use** and **convention-over-configuration** philosophy. It comes with built-in support for request handling, routing, and templating.

To use Rocket, you'll need to include it in your `Cargo.toml`:

toml

```
[dependencies]
rocket = "0.5.0-rc.2"
```

Example of a simple Rocket application:

rust

```
#[macro_use] extern crate rocket;

#[get("/")]
fn index() -> &'static str {
    "Hello, Rocket!"
}

#[launch]
fn rocket() -> _ {
    rocket::build().mount("/", routes![index])
}
```

In this example:

- We define a simple route (/) that returns "Hello, Rocket!".
- #[launch] is used to run the application, and rocket::build() sets up the application with the defined routes.

Rocket is great for quick and easy web development, with support for request guards, templating, and form handling. It's designed to provide a productive development experience, especially for small to medium-sized projects.

Actix:

Actix is another highly popular and powerful web framework for Rust, built on top of the Actix actor framework. It's known for **high performance** and **scalability**. Actix is great for building high-performance web servers and microservices.

To use Actix, add it to `Cargo.toml`:

toml

```toml
[dependencies]
actix-web = "4.0"
tokio = { version = "1", features = ["full"] }
```

Example of a simple Actix web server:

rust

```rust
use actix_web::{web, App, HttpServer};

async fn greet() -> &'static str {
    "Hello, Actix!"
}

#[actix_web::main]
async fn main() -> std::io::Result<()> {
    HttpServer::new(|| {
```

```
        App::new().route("/",
web::get().to(greet))
    })
    .bind("127.0.0.1:8080")?
    .run()
    .await
}
```

In this example:

- We define an asynchronous handler `greet` that returns `"Hello, Actix!"`.
- We set up the web server with `HttpServer::new()` and bind it to `127.0.0.1:8080`.

Actix is a **high-performance framework**, suitable for building scalable and concurrent web applications that can handle a large number of connections and requests.

Building and Deploying a Simple REST API

In this section, we will walk through building a simple **REST API** with **Rocket** or **Actix**, and then discuss how to deploy it.

Example: Building a REST API with Rocket

Let's build a basic REST API using Rocket that allows us to manage a collection of books. We will support creating, retrieving, and listing books.

1. **Add Rocket dependencies:**

Add the following to your `Cargo.toml`:

toml

```
[dependencies]
rocket = "0.5.0-rc.2"
serde = { version = "1.0", features = ["derive"]
}
serde_json = "1.0"
```

2. **Create a Book Model and API Routes:**

rust

```
#[macro_use] extern crate rocket;
use rocket::{State, response::content};
use serde::{Deserialize, Serialize};
use rocket::serde::json::Json;
use std::sync::Mutex;

#[derive(Serialize, Deserialize, Clone)]
```

```
struct Book {
    id: usize,
    title: String,
    author: String,
}


type BookList = Mutex<Vec<Book>>;

#[post("/", data = "<book>")]
fn    create_book(book:    Json<Book>,    state:
&State<BookList>) -> Json<Book> {
    let mut books = state.lock().unwrap();
    books.push(book.into_inner());
    Json(book.into_inner())
}


#[get("/")]
fn    list_books(state:    &State<BookList>)    ->
Json<Vec<Book>> {
    let books = state.lock().unwrap();
    Json(books.clone())
}


#[launch]
fn rocket() -> _ {
    rocket::build()
        .mount("/books",    routes![create_book,
list_books])
```

```
        .manage(Mutex::new(vec![]))    //    Shared
state for books
}
```

Explanation:

- We define a `Book` struct to represent a book.
- We create two routes: one for `POST` `/books` to create a new book, and another for `GET` `/books` to list all books.
- The `State<BookList>` allows us to share mutable state between routes safely using a `Mutex`.
- The application is started with `#[launch]`, and we mount the routes on `/books`.

Run and Test the API:

Run the application with:

```bash
```

```bash
cargo run
```

You can test it with tools like `curl` or Postman.

- **Create a Book:**

```bash
```

```
curl -X POST http://127.0.0.1:8000/books -
H "Content-Type: application/json" -d
'{"id": 1, "title": "Rust Programming",
"author": "John Doe"}'
```

- **List Books:**

```
bash
```

```
curl http://127.0.0.1:8000/books
```

Real-World Example: A Web Application for Real-Time Data

Let's now build a simple web application that handles **real-time data** using **Actix** and **WebSockets**. WebSockets allow for two-way communication between the client and server, which is perfect for real-time applications such as chat apps, stock tickers, or collaborative tools.

1. Add Actix WebSocket dependencies:

In `Cargo.toml`:

```toml
```

```
[dependencies]
actix-web = "4.0"
actix-rt = "2.5"
```

```
tokio = { version = "1", features = ["full"] }
```

2. Set Up the WebSocket Server:

rust

```
use actix_web::{web, App, HttpServer};
use actix_web::web::Bytes;
use actix_web::Error;
use actix_web::HttpResponse;
use actix_web::rt::spawn;
use actix_web::web::Data;
use actix::prelude::*;
use futures_util::{SinkExt, StreamExt};

struct WebSocketSession {
    id: usize,
}

impl WebSocketSession {
    fn new(id: usize) -> Self {
        WebSocketSession { id }
    }
}

async         fn         websocket_handler(ws:
actix_web::web::Data<actix::Addr<WebSocketSessi
on>>) -> Result<HttpResponse, Error> {
    let response = HttpResponse::Ok().finish();
    Ok(response)
}
```

```
#[actix_web::main]
async fn main() -> std::io::Result<()> {
    let             app_data             =
actix::Addr::new(WebSocketSession::new(1));
    HttpServer::new(move || {
        App::new()

.app_data(Data::new(app_data.clone()))
            .route("/ws",
web::get().to(websocket_handler))
    })
    .bind("127.0.0.1:8080")?
    .run()
    .await
}
```

Explanation:

- We define a `WebSocketSession` struct to represent each WebSocket connection.
- We define a `websocket_handler` function that establishes a WebSocket connection and handles the communication.
- The WebSocket server listens on port `8080`.

This basic setup provides the foundation for a real-time communication application, and you can extend it to broadcast messages, handle events, or integrate with front-end frameworks for a complete real-time application.

Conclusion

In this chapter, we've explored **Rust in web development**, focusing on building web applications with **Rocket** and **Actix**. We covered:

- How to set up **Rocket** and **Actix** for building web applications.
- Building and deploying a **REST API** with Rocket.
- Creating a **real-time web application** using **WebSockets** with Actix.

Rust's web development ecosystem is powerful and well-suited for high-performance, scalable applications. As we continue to build and scale web apps, Rust provides the tools and safety guarantees necessary to create fast, reliable, and concurrent web applications. In the next chapter, we'll delve deeper into **security** in Rust and how to secure your web applications against common vulnerabilities.

CHAPTER 17

RUST IN SYSTEMS PROGRAMMING

Rust is a systems programming language that provides fine-grained control over hardware while ensuring safety and concurrency guarantees. This makes it an excellent choice for building **system utilities**, **operating system kernels**, and interacting with low-level components. In this chapter, we will explore **systems programming concepts with Rust**, how to write **system utilities** and **kernels**, and how to interface with **C libraries** using the **Foreign Function Interface (FFI)**. Finally, we will walk through a **real-world example** of building a **custom shell** or **command-line tool** in Rust.

Systems Programming Concepts with Rust

Systems programming involves writing software that interacts directly with hardware or low-level system resources. This includes tasks such as managing memory, interacting with the operating system, and directly handling

I/O devices. Systems programming often requires working with lower-level languages like **C** or **Assembly**.

Rust provides several features that make it suitable for systems programming:

1. **Memory Safety**: Rust's ownership model ensures that memory is managed safely without a garbage collector, preventing common issues like dangling pointers, buffer overflows, and use-after-free errors.

2. **Zero-cost Abstractions**: Rust allows developers to write high-level code without sacrificing performance. It provides abstractions like iterators and closures that have zero overhead after compilation.

3. **Concurrency and Parallelism**: Rust's concurrency model is designed to eliminate race conditions at compile time, making it ideal for systems programming where multiple threads or processes need to operate efficiently and safely.

4. **Low-Level Control**: Rust allows access to low-level operations, such as inline assembly and direct memory manipulation, which is useful for writing system-level software like operating systems, drivers, and other performance-critical applications.

By combining these features, Rust is well-suited for building systems software, especially when safety, concurrency, and performance are crucial.

Writing System Utilities and Operating System Kernels

Rust is increasingly being used for writing system utilities and even **operating system kernels**. Its ability to compile to **bare-metal** code and run without a standard library (i.e., in "no_std" mode) allows developers to write low-level software such as drivers, kernels, and other utilities.

Writing System Utilities:

System utilities are programs or scripts that provide functionality to interact with the system. Examples include file management utilities, process management tools, and network utilities. Rust's performance and control over system resources make it ideal for writing such utilities.

Here's an example of a simple system utility that reads a file and counts the number of words:

```
rust
```

```rust
use std::fs::File;
use std::io::{self, Read};

fn      count_words(file_path:      &str)      ->
io::Result<usize> {
    let mut file = File::open(file_path)?;
    let mut content = String::new();
    file.read_to_string(&mut content)?;
    Ok(content.split_whitespace().count())
}

fn main() {
    match count_words("example.txt") {
        Ok(count) => println!("The file contains
{} words.", count),
        Err(e) => eprintln!("Error: {}", e),
    }
}
```

In this example:

- We define a function count_words that opens a file, reads its content, and counts the number of words.
- The file handling is done using Rust's standard library, ensuring safe and efficient memory management.
- The program runs as a system utility, printing the result or an error.

Writing an Operating System Kernel in Rust:

Rust's ability to run without the standard library (no_std) allows it to be used for **bare-metal programming**, which is the process of writing software that runs directly on hardware, typically for writing operating systems or embedded systems. Writing an operating system kernel in Rust is an advanced topic, but Rust's safety guarantees make it a compelling choice.

Here's an example of a minimal "Hello World" program in Rust for an operating system kernel:

```rust
#![no_std]
#![no_main]

use core::panic::PanicInfo;

#[no_mangle]
pub extern "C" fn _start() -> ! {
    // This is where the kernel code would run.
    // For now, we just loop indefinitely.
    loop {}
}

#[panic_handler]
```

```
fn panic(_info: &PanicInfo) -> ! {
    loop {}
}
```

In this example:

- #![no_std] tells the Rust compiler not to use the standard library, as we are working in an environment that doesn't have it (like a kernel or embedded system).
- The _start function is the entry point for the kernel and is executed when the system boots.
- We also define a panic handler to handle errors during execution.

Building an operating system kernel requires a lot of setup, including bootloading, memory management, and hardware interaction, but Rust's tools and libraries make it possible to write these components with confidence in memory safety and concurrency.

Interfacing with C Libraries Using FFI

Rust's **Foreign Function Interface (FFI)** allows it to call and interact with C code. This is useful when you need to access system-level functionality provided by C libraries or interact with existing C codebases. FFI allows Rust to be integrated with lower-level, system-specific software.

To use FFI in Rust, you need to declare C functions in your Rust code and tell the Rust compiler to link to the corresponding C library.

Using FFI to Call C Code:

Here's an example of calling a C function from Rust:

1. **Write a C function** (in `hello.c`):

c

```c
#include <stdio.h>

void hello_world() {
    printf("Hello from C!\n");
}
```

2. **Create a Rust file to link with the C function**:

rust

```rust
extern "C" {
    fn hello_world();
}
```

```
fn main() {
    unsafe {
        hello_world();  // Calling the C function
    }
}
```

In this example:

- The `extern "C"` block is used to declare a C function (`hello_world`).
- The `unsafe` block is required because calling C functions from Rust is inherently unsafe (since Rust cannot guarantee memory safety when interacting with C code).
- The `hello_world` function will print "Hello from C!" when called.

Building the Project with FFI:

To compile and run this example, follow these steps:

1. Compile the C code:

bash

```
gcc -c hello.c -o hello.o
```

2. Link the C code with the Rust project:

bash

```
rustc main.rs --extern hello=hello.o
```

3. Run the Rust program:

```
bash
```

```
./main
```

This will call the `hello_world` function written in C and print the message from the C code.

Real-World Example: Building a Custom Shell or Command-Line Tool

Rust's performance and safety features make it an excellent choice for building low-level utilities, such as **custom shells** or **command-line tools**. These tools often require efficient I/O handling and process management, and Rust provides robust support for these tasks.

Let's build a simple **custom shell** that accepts user input and runs commands using Rust's `std::process` module.

Example: Building a Simple Shell
```
rust
```

```rust
use std::io::{self, Write};
use std::process::{Command, exit};

fn main() {
    loop {
        print!("> ");
        io::stdout().flush().unwrap();

        let mut input = String::new();
        io::stdin().read_line(&mut input).unwrap();

        let input = input.trim(); // Remove any trailing newlines or spaces

        if input == "exit" {
            break;
        }

        let args: Vec<&str> = input.split_whitespace().collect();

        // Run the command
        let status = Command::new(args[0])
            .args(&args[1..])
            .status()
            .unwrap();
```

```
    if !status.success() {
        eprintln!("Command      failed      with
status: {}", status);
    }
  }

  exit(0);
}
```

Explanation:

- The program continuously prompts the user for input.
- It reads the input, trims it, and then runs the command using `std::process::Command`.
- The shell runs commands like `ls`, `echo`, or any other executable, and exits if the user types `exit`.

Running the Shell:

Compile and run the shell using the following commands:

```
bash
```

```
cargo run
```

Now you can type commands like:

```
shell
```

```
> echo Hello, Rust!
```

211

```
Hello, Rust!
> exit
```

This simple shell demonstrates how to handle user input, execute commands, and manage processes in a system-level program written in Rust.

Conclusion

In this chapter, we explored **Rust in systems programming**, covering key concepts such as:

- **Systems programming** with Rust, including low-level control and memory safety.
- Writing **system utilities** and even **operating system kernels** in Rust.
- Using **FFI** to interface with C libraries and leverage system-level functionality.
- Building a **custom shell** and command-line tool, which is a real-world example of a system utility.

Rust's performance and safety features make it an ideal language for systems programming. Whether you're building operating system kernels, system utilities, or interfacing with low-level libraries, Rust provides the tools necessary to write safe, efficient, and high-performance software. In the next chapter, we will dive deeper into **security** in Rust and discuss how to secure your applications against common vulnerabilities.

CHAPTER 18

ADVANCED RUST TECHNIQUES AND BEST PRACTICES

In this chapter, we will dive deep into **advanced Rust techniques** that give you more control over performance, memory management, and unsafe operations. We will explore advanced patterns like **unsafe Rust**, **zero-cost abstractions**, and discuss **best practices** for writing **idiomatic and efficient Rust code**. Additionally, we'll look at the **future of Rust**, how the language is evolving, and provide a **real-world example** of **large-scale project architecture** in Rust.

Advanced Patterns: Unsafe Rust, Zero-cost Abstractions, and More

Rust provides powerful tools for fine-tuning performance and achieving maximum efficiency. However, these tools often come with trade-offs in terms of safety. Let's explore some advanced patterns that provide more control over your code and allow you to write highly efficient software.

1. Unsafe Rust:

Unsafe Rust is a subset of Rust that allows you to bypass the compiler's safety checks. This is necessary for certain low-level operations that Rust's safe abstractions cannot express, such as interacting directly with hardware, writing low-level data structures, or optimizing performance-critical code.

While **unsafe Rust** allows more flexibility, it also introduces risks, as you must manually ensure memory safety. It is typically used in specific situations like FFI (Foreign Function Interface), manual memory management, or interacting with low-level system APIs.

Here's an example of using unsafe Rust to dereference a raw pointer:

rust

```
fn unsafe_example() {
    let x = 42;
    let r = &x as *const i32; // Create a raw
pointer

    unsafe {
```

```
    println!("Value  of  x:  {}",  *r);  //
Dereferencing the raw pointer
    }
}
```

In this example:

- We create a **raw pointer** using `&x as *const i32`.
- Dereferencing the raw pointer inside an `unsafe` block is allowed because the compiler cannot guarantee that the pointer is valid.

When to use unsafe Rust:

- Interfacing with low-level system code (e.g., writing operating systems, drivers).
- Performing manual memory management (e.g., implementing custom allocators).
- Optimizing performance in specific hot spots where Rust's safe abstractions would introduce unnecessary overhead.

It's important to **minimize the use of unsafe code** and encapsulate it in safe abstractions wherever possible.

2. Zero-Cost Abstractions:

Rust's **zero-cost abstractions** mean that high-level abstractions (like iterators, closures, and async/await) don't incur any performance overhead once compiled. The compiler is capable of optimizing these abstractions into low-level code that is as efficient as manually written code.

For example, an iterator in Rust can be used to express high-level operations like filtering or mapping, but the compiled code will be as efficient as writing a loop by hand.

rust

```
fn sum_of_squares(numbers: Vec<i32>) -> i32 {
    numbers.iter().map(|&x| x * x).sum()
}
```

In this example:

- We use `iter()`, `map()`, and `sum()` to express the computation.
- Rust's optimizer ensures that this code is as efficient as manually written code that performs the same loop.

Zero-cost abstractions allow you to write high-level, expressive code without sacrificing performance, which is one of Rust's most significant features.

3. Memory Layout and Control:

Rust also allows you to control **memory layout** and **alignment**, which is useful when working with low-level code or optimizing data storage. This can be done through **repr(C)** or **repr(align)** attributes, which control how structs are laid out in memory.

rust

```
#[repr(C)]
struct MyStruct {
    a: i32,
    b: f64,
}
```

Using `repr(C)` ensures that the struct's memory layout is compatible with C, which is useful when interfacing with C libraries or writing FFI.

Best Practices for Writing Idiomatic and Efficient Rust Code

To write efficient and idiomatic Rust code, you need to follow certain guidelines and best practices. These practices ensure that your code remains readable, maintainable, and performs well.

1. Use Ownership and Borrowing Properly:

Rust's ownership and borrowing system is the key to memory safety. By using references (&T) and borrowing appropriately, you can avoid unnecessary cloning and ing of data.

```rust
rust

fn print_len(s: &str) {
    println!("Length of string: {}", s.len());
}
```

Here, s is borrowed immutably, and we don't clone or it. This avoids unnecessary memory allocations.

2. Minimize Cloning and Heap Allocations:

While cloning is necessary in certain situations, it's usually better to borrow data instead of cloning it, as cloning can

219

lead to unnecessary allocations. Instead of calling `.clone()` frequently, try to use references wherever possible.

```rust
```

```rust
fn process_data(data: &[u8]) {
    // Process data without cloning it
    let sum: u64 = data.iter().map(|&x| x as
u64).sum();
}
```

3. Use Pattern Matching for Clarity and Efficiency:

Rust's **pattern matching** is one of its most powerful features. Use it to handle different cases cleanly, instead of using long if-else chains. It's also more efficient because it allows the compiler to optimize matching.

```rust
```

```rust
match some_value {
    Some(x) => println!("Got value: {}", x),
    None => println!("No value"),
}
```

This ensures clarity and is optimized by the compiler.

4. Handle Errors with `Result` and `Option`:

Rust provides powerful error handling with the `Result` and `Option` types. Avoid panicking and use these types to handle potential errors gracefully.

rust

```rust
fn divide(a: i32, b: i32) -> Result<i32, String>
{
    if b == 0 {
        Err(String::from("Division by zero"))
    } else {
        Ok(a / b)
    }
}
```

5. Leverage Iterators and Functional Programming:

Rust's iterator-based methods, such as `.map()`, `.filter()`, and `.fold()`, allow you to write more functional code. These methods are not only concise but also allow the compiler to optimize your code at compile time.

rust

```rust
let sum = (1..=10).map(|x| x * 2).sum::<i32>();
```

Rust in the Future: Evolving the Language and Ecosystem

Rust's ecosystem is evolving rapidly, and its future looks bright. Key areas where Rust is continuing to grow include:

- **WebAssembly (Wasm)**: Rust is a popular choice for building WebAssembly applications, as it compiles efficiently to WebAssembly and allows developers to run Rust code in the browser with minimal overhead.
- **Async/Await**: Rust's async model continues to improve, making it easier to write concurrent code that scales efficiently.
- **Embedded Development**: Rust is increasingly being used in embedded systems and **bare-metal programming** due to its safety and performance features.
- **Tooling**: Rust's tooling ecosystem (including `cargo`, `rustfmt`, `clippy`, and `rust-analyzer`) continues to improve, making it easier to write and maintain high-quality code.

As Rust evolves, it will continue to be a powerful tool for systems programming, web development, and embedded systems, with the community driving its growth.

Real-World Example: Large-Scale Project Architecture in Rust

Let's now look at how Rust can be used to architect and build a **large-scale project**. For this example, we'll focus on building a **distributed system** that consists of multiple services interacting with each other, showcasing Rust's strengths in scalability, concurrency, and efficiency.

Project Overview:

We're building a distributed **task queue** system, where different services submit tasks to a central queue, and worker services pull tasks from the queue for processing. The project will consist of:

1. **Task Queue Service**: The central service that accepts incoming tasks from clients and stores them in a queue.
2. **Worker Service**: Worker services that process tasks from the queue concurrently.
3. **API Gateway**: A REST API for interacting with the task queue and monitoring the system.

Service Architecture:

1. **Task Queue Service**:
   o   Handles task submissions via a REST API.

- o Stores tasks in a database or in-memory queue (e.g., `VecDeque`).
- o Exposes an endpoint for workers to pull tasks.

2. **Worker Service**:
   - o Pulls tasks from the task queue service and processes them concurrently.
   - o Uses `tokio` for asynchronous processing and parallel execution.

3. **API Gateway**:
   - o Provides an interface for clients to submit tasks and query the status of the queue.
   - o Built using **Rocket** or **Actix** for high performance and ease of use.

Key Rust Features for This Project:

- **Concurrency**: The project utilizes Rust's async/await model for handling multiple worker threads and services simultaneously.
- **Error Handling**: `Result` and `Option` are used to handle errors gracefully across distributed components.
- **Memory Management**: Rust's ownership model ensures that data is safely shared across services, and resources like task queues are managed without race conditions.

Conclusion

In this chapter, we explored **advanced Rust techniques** for systems programming, including:

- **Unsafe Rust, zero-cost abstractions**, and advanced patterns.
- **Best practices** for writing idiomatic and efficient Rust code, including memory management and error handling.
- The **future of Rust** and how it is evolving to support new paradigms like **WebAssembly, async programming**, and **embedded development**.
- A **real-world example** of a **large-scale project architecture** in Rust, showcasing the power of Rust in building distributed systems.

Rust is a powerful language for systems programming, and its safety, performance, and concurrency features make it ideal for both low-level system utilities and large-scale applications. As Rust continues to evolve, it will only become more integral to high-performance, reliable software.

www.ingramcontent.com/pod-product-compliance
Lightning Source LLC
LaVergne TN
LVHW051324050326
832903LV00031B/3348